KING'S HALL AND MERTON 1712

A HISTORY

OF

THE PARISHES OF

MINCHINHAMPTON

AND

AVENING

BY

ARTHUR TWISDEN PLAYNE, B.A.

Forsan et hœc olim meminisse juvabit.

Virgil A. 1, 203

ALAN SUTTON
1978

First published 1915
This edition published by Alan Sutton 1978,
with a new introduction by Geoffrey Sanders.

ISBN 0 904387 25 9

Printed in Great Britain by Redwood Burn Limited,
Trowbridge & Esher
Bound by Cedric Chivers Limited, Bath

PREFACE

THE greater part of the following account of the Parishes which form the subject of this short History was contributed in monthly papers to the Minchinhampton Parish Magazine during the year 1913 and part of 1914. These intervals of writing caused the story I had to tell to be somewhat disjointed, and exigences of space also made it necessary to keep out a considerable amount of matter which should have found a place in the text. At the request of many residents in the two Parishes, I have collected these monthly parts, rearranging them, and including some additional facts which I had been obliged to omit. The Illustrations, which did not appear in the Parish Magazine, are also included, and will, I hope, add to the interest of the Book.

I have always thought that some account should be written of every Parish, to supplement the County Histories, which can naturally only deal with main facts, and there is scarcely a Parish in England which does not possess some features of interest worthy of record. No connected story of the two Parishes of Minchinhampton and Avening has yet appeared, and it is with the hope of supplying this omission that I have ventured to publish this little History.

I take this opportunity of expressing my indebtedness to many who have helped me in producing this book. My thanks are especially due to Mr Roland Austin for most kindly undertaking the labour of compiling the Index, and for reading and correcting the proofs. I desire also to record my thanks to Mr A. E. Dickinson, who most generously placed at my disposal his large collection of extracts relating to the history of the two Parishes, thereby saving me much labour and research, and to Mr and Mrs Sidney Webb for allowing me to quote from their " History of English Local Government,'' including " The Story of the King's Highway.'' To Mr Thomas Falconer I am indebted for rubbings taken of the Brasses in Minchinhampton Church, and also for a sketch of Dame Alice Hampton's Bell. To Mr A. E. Smith for kindly contributing his Paper on the Geology of the district, containing a great amount of information in a narrow compass My thanks are also due to Mr F. A. Hyett and Mr St. Clair Baddeley for much help and encouragement.

The Illustrations are engraved by Mr Emery Walker, whose name is a guarantee for excellence of workmanship, and I am also indebted to Messrs Bellows for the careful manner in which the printing and other details of the Book have been carried out.

CONTENTS

LIST OF ILLUSTRATIONS

INTRODUCTION TO THE
1978 EDITION

"A History of the Parishes of Minchinhampton and Avening" by Arthur Twisden Playne of Longfords House, Minchinhampton, was published in 1915 after the greater part had appeared as monthly papers to the Minchinhampton Parish Magazine during the year 1913 and part of 1914.

The Playne family, originally refugees or immigrants from the Netherlands, settled in Kent about the middle of the sixteenth century, but about the year 1650 they disappeared from that county to establish themselves in Gloucestershire as clothiers. In 1759 Thomas Playne, great-grandfather of Arthur Playne, bought Frogmarsh Mill in the parish of Woodchester — he lived at Sourwell (or Summer Well), which was later incorporated in the Convent — and before his death in 1788 he disposed of these properties on purchasing Longfords. Here was to be the hub of the family's acquisitions in the parishes of Minchinhampton and Avening.

Longfords lies in the parish of Minchinhampton between Avening (where Thomas Playne's son acquired the Manor) and Nailsworth, and to the north-west across the fields the family interests included Box House, as well as Forwood Brewery and the adjacent Springfield on the outskirts of Minchinhampton.

Thomas Playne was followed by William I (1772-1850) and William II (1804-1884) and then by his great-grandson Arthur (1843-1923), who in 1870 married Mary Elizabeth, the third of the nine daughters of Richard Potter of Standish Park, Glos., chairman of the Great Western Railway Co. She was the founder of the Gloucester College of Domestic Science and her eight sisters were: Laurencina (wife of Robert Holt, a great shipowner and first Lord Mayor of Liverpool), Catherine (wife of Lord Courtney of Penwith), Georgina (wife of D. Meinertzhagen, stockbroker), Blanche (wife of W. Harrison Cripps, a famous surgeon), Theresa (wife of Charles Alfred Cripps, Q.C., M.P. for Stroud and afterwards Lord Parmoor), Margaret Heyworth (wife of Henry Hobhouse, chairman of Somerset County Council for 20 years), Rosalind Heyworth (wife of Arthur D. Williams) and Beatrice (wife of Sidney Webb, afterwards Lord Passfield, with whose political interests she was closely associated).

Having married into this brilliant family, Arthur Playne himself was no less gifted. Educated at Brasenose College, Oxford, not only was he the very successful chairman of the family firm, but in his lifetime he was an alderman of the County Council, chairman of the Nailsworth bench of magistrates, a leader of the Conservative Party who helped considerably to secure the return of his brother-in-law, Charles Cripps, as Member of Parliament for Stroud in 1895, and the one through whose efforts the institution of the Minchinhampton Golf Club was mainly due (he, incidentally, owned the Old Lodge Inn, headquarters of the Club, as well as the Weighbridge Inn near his home).

The family fortunes had been begun by Arthur Playne's great-grandfather Thomas, but, as we shall read in Chapter XXI, when he died in 1788 his affairs were in a state of confusion. The firm, however, was reconstituted under the name of his widow. Martha Playne (1747-1824) — she brought up a large family of eleven children — and their eldest son William I. Martha Wakeley, as she was before her marriage in 1773, had been Thomas's housekeeper and the eldest son was born out of wedlock in 1772.

In 1797 Martha retired and the business became William Playne and Co. In 1801 Peter Playne.(d. 1851), the first legitimate child, entered the firm, which now became known as William and Peter Playne. There were frequent quarrels due to the elder brother's illegitimacy and after their mother's death Peter set up at Dunkirk Mill, which he later ran with his son Charles of Theescombe, Amberley. Peter himself owned Box House.

Charles Playne took a great interest in the history of the locality and made a study of the Woodchester Roman Pavement, on which he addressed the Bristol and Gloucestershire Archaeological Society when they visited Stroud in 1885, and Minchinhampton Common formed the subject of an earlier lecture to the Nailsworth Literary and Mechanics Institute in 1874 (in the latter he firmly stated that Tom Long's name had been given to the cross roads on Minchinhampton Common as the site of the burial of this poor suicide at the beginning of the 19th century, an event then close enough in memory as to be authentic).

Another relation of Arthur Playne, George F. Playne, F.G.S., of Whitecroft, Nailsworth, who died at Stuttgart in 1879 at the early age of 55, had a wide reputation as an antiquarian, and Gloucester City Public Library contains eight examples of his work, including one on ancient encampments in Gloucestershire. It is probable that Charles and George Playne fostered Arthur's interest in the history of his neighbourhood. His first incursion was to give a paper on Avening Church to the county Archaeological Society at a special meeting in Stroud on February 4th 1889. The meeting had its humourous side, for at the conclusion of the lecture up jumped the rector of Avening, the Rev. F. de Paravicinci, who said that he, too, proposed to read his paper on his church. However, the chairman, Sir John Dorington, ruled that no notice had been given of the rector's intention, that the hour was late and that the paper could not be admitted.

There was another younger brother of William I, whose branch was to play an important part in the Playne saga. He was George (1779-1847), who built Springfield in 1809 and founded the Minchinhampton Brewery at Forwood. By 1890 the Brewery owned or leased 27 licensed houses, mainly in Minchinhampton but as far afield as Bisley and Wotton-under-Edge. George Playne's grandson Edward (1843-1907), first chairman of the Stroud Rural District Council 1894-1907, sold the firm to Stroud Brewery in 1897 and later became its managing director.

Arthur Playne's mother, Mary Anne, daughter of Joseph Ellis-Viner of Badgeworth Court, married his father, William II, in 1836 and in 1868 she was tragically killed in a carriage accident. The east end window in the chancel of Minchinhampton Church is dedicated in her memory. In 1871 William II was High Sheriff of Gloucestershire and on his death in 1884 the Longfords estate passed to Arthur. The elder son, Captain Frederick Carl Playne of the Rifle Brigade, had died in 1863 and his daughter Mary Viner, who married Robert Erskine Pollock, Q.C., inherited Avening Court and the manorial rights, which William I had acquired from Philip Sheppard in 1813 and which remained in the family until about 1920.

After Arthur's death in 1923 the Longfords estate passed to his son Lt.-Col. William Heyworth Playne, who had been badly wounded at Gallipoli in the first World War. His cousin Herbert Clement Playne (1870-1943) of Box House and Springfield, who was headmaster of Bancrofts School 1905-31, succeeded him in

1935. The great-grandson of the founder of the Brewery, he was the father of Edward Playne, D.S.C., F.R.I.B.A., the present owner of Springfield.

Longfords House has now become a Community Home School for Girls and the mills, once part of a local consortium, have been taken over by the Illingworth Morris Group of Yorkshire.

From the days of Thomas Playne there have been many fluctuations in the family and, as Arthur Twisden Playne has shown, it has played a considerable part in the history of the parishes of Minchinhampton and Avening. A reviewer of the first edition of the history so truly said that "Mr. Playne's hope that the book will be of interest to those who live in the neighbourhood is sure to be fulfilled". This second edition provides further opportunity for fulfilment of that hope.

Geoffrey Sanders,

Bisley, 1978

CHAPTER I.

INTRODUCTION

THE two parishes of Minchinhampton and Avening have been so closely associated from early times that it is scarcely possible to separate the history of the one from that of the other. The two manors have been held together continuously by successive owners from the Conquest to the early part of the 19th century, a period of nearly 800 years, and, therefore, I have thought that it would give rise to less confusion to give an account of both these parishes, whose history has been so intimately connected from earliest times.

Though such close neighbours, each of the two parishes has its own distinctive features in situation and environment. The town of Minchinhampton stands on a broad plateau, which is a spur of the Cotswolds, upwards of 600 ft. above sea level, and overlooking the broad valley of the Severn to the Welsh hills beyond on one side, and on the other is the long range of Wiltshire hills, where on clear days the monument on the height above the town of Calne is to be seen. The ancient parish was bounded on the north by the little river Frome, which, rising in the Sapperton hills, flows through the " Golden Valley," where the Great Western Railway now winds its way from Swindon to Gloucester, finally joining the broad waters of the Severn and giving its name in passing to Frampton and Framilode. It is bounded on the south by the Avening brook, which, flowing through what is now Longfords Lake, ultimately joins the Frome near Dudbridge ; on the east by the parish of Sapperton, beyond which is the town of Cirencester, the capital of the Cotswolds, and on the west by the parish of Rodborough, which was formerly part of Minchinhampton.

The village of Avening, on the other hand, lies in one of
the lovely valleys which run from the Severn Vale up into the
hills, each contributing its little rivulet to swell the volume of
the great river ; and, of all these valleys, that in which Avening
is situated is one of the most beautiful.

The parish of Avening is bounded on the north by the
sister parish of Minchinhampton until it meets the parish of
Woodchester at Inchbrook.   It included part of the small town
of Nailsworth, where it is squeezed into very narrow limits by
the parishes of Minchinhampton and Horsley, but expands
again on leaving the town and meets successively the parishes
of Woodchester and Nympsfield on the west and those of
Beverston, Tetbury and Cherington on the south and east.

Both parishes were densely wooded in ancient times.   In
Minchinhampton, Gatcombe wood was considerably larger than
it is now, much of the land on the high level ground having
been brought under cultivation.   Hazelwood in Avening parish
is also smaller than it once was, some 300 acres having been
cleared and cultivated, principally by Mr William Playne,
senior.   Hazelwood was part of a large forest which stretched
over Horsley, Kingscote and Woodchester, and clothed the
sides of the hills overlooking the Severn Vale far beyond the
limits of our two parishes.   There were occasional clearings
and open country round the villages and at other points, as,
for instance, at " Forest Green," now part of the town of
Nailsworth, which still retains its ancient name.   The prevailing trees in this forest were beech, though in suitable soil
there was a considerable quantity of oak and also a certain
amount of ash and sycamore.   In modern times larch has been
planted over a large extent, especially on the hillsides after
the felling of the beech.   The early foliage of the latter tree
and its golden tints in autumn are most beautiful, and the
winding road through the woods between Nailsworth and
Avening with Longfords Lake below is justly famed for its
beauty.

The inhabitants of the two parishes have, as a rule, from
early times been healthy, well fed and well housed.   Work has
been plentiful for those willing to do it, and wages, especially
in the mills, have been good, and unemployment rare.   The
cottages are of the usual substantial Cotswold type, stone
built and stone tiled, though I regret to say that brick and

slate tiles are yearly coming more into evidence, and I fear the jerry builder is not unknown, though recent legislation has largely curbed his activities. Almost all cottages have ample gardens attached to them, and where this is not possible, allotments are easily obtainable. Taken altogether there are worse places to live in than within the bounds of the ancient parishes of Minchinhampton and Avening.

PREHISTORIC MAN.

There are many evidences in both parishes of the very early existence of man, and though there are but few traces remaining of the earliest or palæolithic man, he was, no doubt, an inhabitant of Britain when it was united to the Continent. But his remains have disappeared during the great glacial periods, which occurred in times so remote that we can form no conception of their extent or duration. Many of these glacial periods occurred when England, Scandinavia, North Germany and many parts of France were tight locked in Arctic ice, and man had to migrate to more genial climates. Professor Geikie says[1] : "After the great *mer de glace*, which extended from Scandinavia to the plains of Germany . . . . had melted away, vegetation followed the retreating steps of the ice, and palæolithic man, accompanied by the Arctic mammalia, wandered over Europe. As the climate grew milder these latter migrated northward and were succeeded by the temperate and southern groups. This period of mild and genial winters passed away, but before it did so a large part of the British islands disappeared below the sea. As this submergence continued the last glacial epoch began. The land again rose, and great confluent glaciers covered a large part of the British islands and Scandinavia. Eventually the ice retired and then Britain for the last time became continental. As years rolled on the sea again stole in between our islands and the Continent until a final severance was effected. From early neolithic times a gradual improvement and progress attended the efforts of our barbaric predecessors until at length a period arrived when men began to abandon the use of stone implements and weapons and for them to substitute bronze. And so, passing on through the age of bronze and the days of the builders of Stonehenge, we are at last brought face to face with the age of iron and the dawn of history."

[1] "The Great Ice Age," pp. 552–554.

Both parishes are rich in remains of neolithic man. His " barrows " or burying places, are plentifully strewn over the hills, as at Gatcombe, on Minchinhampton Common, and on the Copse at Avening ; and the remains of pit dwellings on the Common and elsewhere show the places where he lived. Many flint implements are found in the vicinity of ancient British camps, notably at " Rugger's Green," in the parish of Avening, where great quantities of flint weapons have been found and are still to be seen whenever the neighbouring fields are ploughed up. In addition to the tumuli there are two very remarkable monuments belonging to the Stone Age. One is a very fine monolith, locally called the " Long Stone," on the left hand side of the main road a short distance from Gatcombe Lodge entrance. It is 7½ ft. high above the ground, and is said to be as much below the surface. It is a very fine block of the peculiar stratum of the great oolite formation, locally called holey stone, which underlies the surface soil to a thickness varying from 6"—18". Report says that the superstitious mothers were in the habit of passing ricketty children through a hole in this stone with the idea that they would by such means become strong. A much smaller stone of a similar kind stands in a wall about 30 ft. away, and a third is said to have been removed during the last century.

There is a very remarkable tumulus a few hundred yards south of the Long Stone, which, on being opened in the year 1870, was found to contain a sepulchral chamber 8 ft. long, 4 ft. wide, and 5 ft. 6 in. high, with an entrance porch 3 ft. square and covered by a massive stone 9 ft. 6 ins. long and 5 ft. 6 ins. wide. In this sepulchral chamber was found a skeleton in a sitting position at the farthest end. Another very interesting tumulus is also at Gatcombe, though in Avening parish, and is said by Mr G. F. Playne to be the only example in the district of a *crowned* barrow, having on its summit a very large stone which formerly stood upright, called the " Tinglestone." These and other remains show that this neighbourhood was a favourite place of residence for a considerable number of our early ancestors.

CHAPTER II.

NOTES ON THE GEOLOGY OF MINCHINHAMPTON

By ALFRED EDWARD SMITH.

"VOSSOLS! What be they, Wurr'ms?" About 50 years ago a searcher for geological specimens on a bank outside Balls Green Quarry, Box Common, Minchinhampton, was asked the above question by an old man who was curious to know what was being looked for.

During the last half century geological knowledge has spread widely, but there may be still a few Minchinhampton parishioners left who might find it difficult to give even an outline of the geological formation of their district, and the object of these few notes is to assist them to do so. The abundance and variety of the fossils, and the interesting nature of the strata, render this parish one of the best in the County for a student of geology to commence his acquaintance with a most fascinating and useful branch of natural history.

The Pioneer of the study of the local Geology was the late Dr John Lycett, who lived and worked at Minchinhampton for many years, and whose book on the " Geology of the Cotswold Hills," published in 1857, is still a foundation work for all who seek to know something of the Geology of this district. Dr. Lycett spent much time in collecting and naming the fossils then found in the neighbourhood, especially in the Great Oolite Quarries on Minchinhampton Common, and he enriched the British Museum and the Cambridge University Museum with the results of his labours.

Since his time the late Mr G. F. Playne, F.G.S., of Nailsworth, and the late Mr Edwin Witchell, F.G.S., of Stroud, have worked in the same district, and have contributed many valuable papers on the subject to the Proceedings of the Cotswold Field Club. Mr Edwin Witchell published in 1882 a

little work called " The Geology of Stroud," which, though
based on Mr Lycett's book, carries local geological knowledge
to more recent times.   It is from Mr Witchell's work that
the following outline sketch of Minchinhampton Geology is
mainly derived, but Mr G. F. Playne's Section of the strata
under Minchinhampton Common, printed with this paper, will
be found of great assistance and will save much description.

Looking at this Section it will be seen that any one standing
near the centre of Minchinhampton Common has under his
feet, until the level of the bottom of the valleys on either side
is reached, four divisions or beds of rock, clay, and sand, in the
following descending order :—

No. on Section.		Thickness about.
7.	Rock—Great Oolite (" Weather Stone," etc.)	100
6.	Clay—Fullers' Earth	70
5.	Rock—Inferior Oolite (Freestone, etc.) ..	180
4.	Sands—Cotteswold Sands	100
	Total ..	450 ft.

The above figures are only approximate, as the beds vary in
thickness.

These four beds rest on the blue Upper Lias clay, the
upper portion of which forms the floor of the Valleys at Nailsworth and Brimscombe.   Both the two beds of rock, Nos. 7
and 5, have many sub-divisions, but these latter are outside
the limits of this chapter.

Taking the four beds mentioned above in order, the chief
feature of No. 7 (the Great Oolite) is the well-known Minchin-
hampton-Common Building or Weather Stone, renowned for
its strength and hardness, and its ability to withstand all
weather.   Some of its sub-divisions are full of fossils, and it
was chiefly from the quarries on Minchinhampton Common
that the late Dr Lycett obtained the many beautiful specimens
which he supplied to the British and Cambridge University
Museums, and a few of which are figured in Plate VII. of his
book on the Cotswold Hills.   A letter of Dr Lycett's, dated
13th February, 1843, to Mr W. Pearse, of Minchinhampton,
asks the latter to take a small basket of fossils to the coach
office and book it to Cambridge ; the basket was directed to
" Rev. Professor Sedgwick, University of Cambridge."

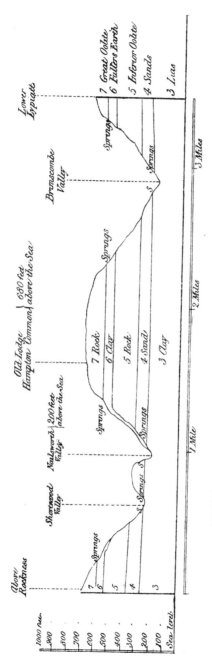

SECTION OF THE HILLS NEAR NAILSWORTH, GLOUCESTERSHIRE

The following quotation from Mr E. Witchell's book, as to the origin of fossils, is applicable to the Great Oolite bed No. 7, and will give in a condensed form a reply to the question at the head of this Chapter—" What be they ? "

" The Geologist, examining for the first time a bed of rock, " finds it composed mainly of fossils ; he sees that the strata " above and below are comparatively unfossiliferous ; he con- " cludes that he is looking upon the remains of a life-period " in the history of the earth ; that in the stratum before him " are the remains of once living creatures that existed in the " sea in which that stratum was deposited. He finds on " further investigation that many of these creatures dis- " appeared when the deposition came to an end and the con- " ditions changed, while some survived and passed into the " next formation ; that with subsequent deposits new species " appeared, something like the former, though not identically " the same, but occupying their place with those which had " survived, and so on through succeeding formations, thus " preserving the continuity of life and giving birth to the " multitudinous species that make up the earth's life-history.' '

No. 6 Bed (the Fullers' Earth Clay) is of great importance to the parish of Minchinhampton, as without it there would be no water on the sides of the hills in this district ; the clay beds of the Fullers' Earth, however, retain and throw out in the form of springs on the sides of the hills the water which per-colates through the rocky beds of the Great Oolite. These springs are seen at Amberley, Box, Forwood, Well Hill and other places on about the same level ; in fact, but for these Fullers' Earth Clay Springs there would have been no such places as Amberley and the Box, because no houses would have been built so far from water. These high level springs are nearly pure, except from lime, which makes the water hard.

The old practice, now it is to be hoped discontinued, of draining the houses built on the Great Oolite into fissures (locally called " lissens ") of that rock, was a frequent source of the pollution of the wells and springs in the Fullers' Earth, and a great danger to the health of the public.

In places this Fullers' Earth Clay has slipped down the sides of the valleys and covered the light soil of the Inferior Oolite below with a deep and more fertile one, so that in some hillside orchards the extent of the slip can be guessed by the increased size of the trees growing on the Fullers' Earth, compared with those growing on the lighter soil of the Inferior Oolite. At the same time these clay slips are highly dangerous to build on, as they are liable to move after a long spell of dry weather followed by heavy rain, and also in consequence of their base being cut into. An example of the former is the case of the first stone house built at the Highlands, and one of the latter occurred at Dyehouse Mills, when the Railway was cut through a Fullers' Earth Slip and started a movement which extended up the hill towards Amberley. This caused the downfall of a house just above the Railway, in which the late Mr G. F. Tabram then lived; when it began he used to take a hatchet and saw to bed with him, to cut open his bedroom door in the morning after it had jammed in the night. These clay slips appear, from sections seen of them when cut across, to have been a succession of slips one over the other extending over long periods. A modern small one, which took place about 30 or 40 years ago, can be seen on the Hazelwood side of the Nailsworth Valley, opposite Scar Hill.

All the wells sunk in the Great Oolite had to go down through that rock until the clay bed of the Fullers' Earth which retained the water was reached, and in former days some persons for want of a little geological knowledge, lost all the water in their wells by thinking that they would get more by going deeper, instead of which they let the water out by going through the bottom of the Fullers' Earth bed into the stony and pervious rock of the Inferior Oolite below, which is bed No. 5 in the above List and Section.

The most important and valuable portion of the Inferior Oolite is the Building Freestone, which is quarried by tunnelling into the side of the hill in galleries extending in some cases, as at Balls Green, for more than a mile. This stone is formed of small round egg-like grains cemented together and appropriately described as *Oolite* from the Greek word *öon* (egg), and *lithos* (stone), eggstone. In a cubic inch of freestone in which the grains are of ordinary size they have been estimated to number not less than 14,000. This fine-grained white freestone is more adapted for the interior of buildings than the exterior. A few beds or sub-divisions yield stone which when properly dried before use will stand the weather, but the general character of the rock is too porous and absorbent of water for external use. The changes of weather in winter materially affect the walls of houses built of this stone, and occasionally, when a sudden change takes place, the inner surface of the walls becomes wet. The Balls Green Quarry before mentioned provided the stone for a great part of the interior work of the Houses of Parliament, and lately a large quantity from this Quarry has been used in the construction of the new G.W.R. Station at Exeter.

Above the Building Freestone are several beds of hard Ragstone, which have been extensively used for road stone and dry walling.

The base of the Inferior Oolite rests on Bed No. 4, called the Cotswold Sands, sections of which may be seen on the Pensile Road leading from Nailsworth to Minchinhampton, at Holcombe Mill, and at the bottom of the Iron Mills Hill. These sands act as a filter for the water, which, by faults and slips gets through the three upper beds, and is then thrown out by the Upper Lias Clay at the base of the Sands. The water in these Springs is abundant and beautifully pure, it is not affected by sudden outbursts after continuous rains (as in the case of the Springs in the Fullers' Earth), but maintains its quantity and temperature equally in summer and winter. The water power of the Mills in the Valleys is mainly supplied by the springs from the base of these sands.

The junction of the Cotswold Sands with the Upper Lias Clay is at Nailsworth, just 230 feet above sea level. The highest point on Minchinhampton Common is 680 feet, and the 450 feet difference in height is made up by the thickness of the four beds above described.

The Lias formation below the Valleys extends about 800 feet down, and is, therefore, too deep a subject for the limits of this paper.

Many beautiful and interesting fossils are found in the Great Oolite and in the Inferior Oolite beds. There is a small but well-arranged collection of these, made by the late Mr G. F. Playne, in the Nailsworth Institute Reading Room, and when the Stroud Museum is completed, it is to be hoped that a representative Collection of the local fossils will be obtained for Exhibition and Study there.

On this subject the following words by the late Mr Edwin Witchell, F.G.S., written in 1882, may be a useful reminder to those concerned :—

" There is no known place in Europe in which the Great " Oolite is so fossiliferous as in the vicinity of Stroud, and yet " the Geologist has to go to distant towns to see the fossils " obtained from this locality. It is hoped that this state of " things will not be of long continuance."

In conclusion the writer hopes that the above scanty outline of Minchinhampton Geology will be sufficient to show that some little knowledge of local Geology may be both useful and interesting.

CHAPTER III.

THE ROMAN OCCUPATION.

THE first attempt to conquer Britain was made by Julius Caesar, who landed with a small force on the coast of Kent in the year 55 B.C., but owing to the opposition of the inhabitants and the scattering of his ships by a severe storm, he did not penetrate far inland. During the following year he came again with an army of 30,000 men, and advanced some distance into the interior, defeating a few tribes and receiving the submission of others. But after a stay of about two months he left the country and returned to Gaul. After an interval of nearly 100 years the final conquest of Britain was undertaken by the Emperor Claudius, who landed on the south coast with an army of 40,000 men. Being called back to Rome, Claudius handed over the command of the expedition to a distinguished general, Aulus Plautius, who was the real conqueror of Britain. There are many evidences of the presence of the Romans in the district in which our two parishes lie, and there may be still a villa to be discovered in Gatcombe Wood or Hazelwood. On altering the course of the old pack-horse road leading through Hazelwood, a Roman votive altar was found, and is now in the possession of the writer at Longfords. It is in excellent preservation, and has a figure of Mars with shield and spear cut in bold relief upon it.

Even before the conquest and occupation by the Romans, there had been considerable intercourse between Britain and the Continent ; Roman settlers had already begun to make their homes in Britain and the ancient inhabitants had by this means become considerably more civilised. But it is not within our province to go deeply into the history of the Roman Conquest and occupation, and we can only glance at a few facts affecting our immediate subject.

There is no doubt that Gloucestershire played a part in the Roman scheme of conquest and colonisation. The many beautiful villas within the county, notably at Woodchester, Chedworth, and Witcomb, prove that it was a favourite place of residence for the wealthy Romans. Besides being pleasant as a home, the county was also strategically most important on account of the broad waters of the Severn and the steep escarpment of the Cotswolds, both river and hills being easily defensible against the incursions of the wild tribes of Wales. The main military road from Corinium (Cirencester) to Glevum (Gloucester) passed through the present site of Minchinhampton, and often must the celebrated 2nd legion under Vespasian the lieutenant of the general Aulus Plautius, and afterwards Emperor, have passed, in stately march, from Corinium over what is now Hampton Common down into the valley to the banks of the Severn.

The Roman occupation lasted until about the end of the 4th century, when there was a gradual withdrawal of the garrisons, every man being required for the defence of Rome. Many Roman settlers still remained, chiefly in cities such as Silchester, but central government ceased to exist and a period of anarchy ensued. Moreover, by the Teutonic conquest of Gaul, Britain became isolated and exposed to piratical raids in the south and to incursions by the Picts and Scots in the north.

THE SAXONS AND THE DANES.

Unfortunately, the Saxon chronicles are vague and confused and it is difficult to form a clear conception of events from the end of the Roman occupation until a short time before the Norman conquest. There is specially little to be recorded as to our two parishes until the first Danish invasion. The following passage relating to Minchinhampton is taken from Bigland's Gloucestershire :—

"A very furious battle was fought in A.D. 628 between Penda King of Mercia and his rebellious sons Cynegils and Cwichelm near Cirencester ; nor are there vestiges of Saxon entrenchments nearer than these (*i.e.*, on Minchinhampton Common). In succeeding centuries the Danes when landing on this side of the Severn proceeded to higher grounds, marking their progress by the most cruel devastation. In one of these predatory incursions in A.D. 918, during the reign of Edward

the Elder, it is recorded in the Saxon Chronicle ' that the inhabitants of Herefordshire rose in arms, and, being joined by
those of Gloucestershire, they fell upon the Danes, and after
a bloody battle put them to flight with the loss of Harold,
one of their leaders.' Edward is said to have encamped on
this side of the Severn, and, although the name ' Woeful
Dane bottom ' may be allusive to some fatal overthrow of
the robbers, the other bulwarks must have been necessary to
protect the inhabitants from their frequent attacks, of which
they lived in constant dread." Thus far Bigland.

The legend of ' Woeful Dane bottom ' has been further
embellished in more recent times and firmly believed in.
According to the most popular version the Danes are said to
have marched by the " Daneway " and were met by the
Saxons at Woeful Dane. The slaughter of the Danes was so
great that the blood came up over the fetlocks of the Saxon
horses. I am sorry to throw doubt on so picturesque a legend,
but the " Daneway " has nothing to do with the Danes, and is
simply " Dene-weg," the valley way. With regard to Woeful
Dane, Mr St. Clair Baddeley says : " Dane is a not-uncommon
transformation of ' Den : ' Anglo-saxon ' dene : ' a valley ;
the prefix probably stands for the personal name ' Wulff-
læd.' The complete form would thus be Wulfflæd-dene-
bottom.[1] "

There was a large Danish garrison at Cirencester, and it is
reasonable to suppose that they would not have neglected so
advantageous an outpost as that afforded by Minchinhampton
Common. In 894 a decisive victory over the Danes was
gained by King Ethelred at a place supposed to be Tidenham,
at the junction of the Severn and the Wye, and, in consequence
of that victory, this part of Gloucestershire become free from
these marauders, though the Danes were not finally conquered
till about the year 925.

There is an interesting Saxon Charter connected with the
parish of Avening, which until recently included Nailsworth,
preserved in one of the Cottonian MSS. in the British Museum,
of which the following is a translation :—

" In the name of the Holy Trinity. Since the Apostle
says we brought nothing into the world nor can we take anything out ; therefore, on account of this I, Athebald, King

---

[1] " Place-names of Gloucestershire," p. 166.

of the Southern Saxons, considering the shortness of my life and that with these perishable things are to be purchased the eternal kingdom of heaven, and being asked by the venerable Bishop Wilfred, I grant in perpetuity most willingly the full right of possession to the Church of the Holy Apostle Peter within the City of Worcester, woodland to the extent of three cassates (*i.e.*, a house with land sufficient to maintain a family) of wooded country in the place called in the ancient speech Woodchester, with these ordained boundaries : on the north Rodenbeorg (Rodborough) ; on the east Smiccumbe (Theescombe) ; on the south Senedberg (Sugley) ; Hardanleag (Harley wood) Neglesleag Minor (Little Nailsworth) ; on the west Haesburgh and Haboucumb ; " the two last names may be Hazelwood and Holcombe, but the points of the compass do not agree.

CHAPTER IV.

THE TWO MANORS AT THE TIME OF THE
NORMAN CONQUEST

I N the reign of Edward the Confessor, the Manor of Minchinhampton was held by Goda, wife of Eustace Count of
Boulogne, and sister of the King, in whose possession it remained till the Norman Conquest. It was then confiscated,
and a few years later given to the Convent of the Holy Trinity
at Caen, called " L'Abbaye aux Dames," which had recently
been founded by Queen Matilda, William at the same time
founding the Church and Monastery of St. Etienne called
" L'Abbaye aux Hommes ;" also at Caen. The following is
the Deed of Gift translated from the original Latin.

" Whoever, for the benefit of the Holy Church of God,
any portion of his own things has bestowed, in the
Heavenly Kingdom by the highest Retributor, we by no
means doubt shall be recompensed. Wherefore, I,
William, King of the English and chief of the Normans
and the Cenomani,[1] together with my wife Queen Matilda,
daughter of Baldwin Duke of Flanders, and niece of Henry,
most illustrious King of the French, do give and for ever
concede to the Church of the Holy Trinity which, for the
salvation of our souls, we have jointly built in the territory
of Caen, these underwritten Manors with all their appertenances as free and quiet as they were in the last days of
King Edward's life—namely (in England) Felsted in the
County of Essex, Hampton and Pinbury in the County of
Gloucester, Tarrant in the County of Dorset. This
chapter we confirm on both sides by our authority and by

[1] The Cenomani inhabited the duchy of Maine, which was conquered and annexed by William.

that of our Bishops and Grandees in the year of our Lord 1082, by declaration due on the condition that, if anyone shall dare to encroach on or take away anything, he shall be cut off from Orthodox Communion and incur the wrath of Almighty God."

signum Willelmi Anglorum regis
signum Comitis Roberti Moritonii
signum Lanfranci Archiepiscopi
signum Matildis reginæ
signum Roberti Comitis filii regis
signum Wacheli episcopi

signum Henrici filii regis	signum Henrici de Ferieres
signum Willelmi de Bracosa	signum Edwardi Vicecomes
signum Stigandi episcopi	signum Hugoni de Pertu
signum Alani Comitis	signum Rogerii Bigot
signum Willelmi de Varenna	signum Hugoni Comitis de
signum Rogeri Comitis de	Cestra
Montegomerii	

This was a cheap gift of William's, seeing that these manors had been taken without payment from their Saxon possessors, as in the case of Hampton, which, as already mentioned, formerly belonged to the Saxon Countess Goda. It is perhaps permissible to doubt whether he will ultimately be recompensed in the manner he desired for this gift which cost him nothing.

The Manor of Avening formed part of the vast possessions of the great Thane Brictric, son of Algar, who was descended from the Saxon Kings. As the story goes he fell under the displeasure of Queen Matilda, whose hand in marriage he had refused when Ambassador at the Court of her father, Baldwin Duke of Flanders. This insult she is said never to have forgiven, and she appears to have persuaded her husband to dispossess Brictric of all his lands, and, amongst others, of the Manor of Avening, which was transferred, together with Minchinhampton, to the recently established Convent of Caen. I have not been able to discover the original Deed of Gift of the Manor of Avening, but it is reasonable to suppose that it was granted about the same time and on the same terms as the Manor of Minchinhampton. Of the subsequent history of Brictric we know little. He was arrested at Tewkesbury, where he formerly had large possessions, but how long he remained in

prison is not stated.   After the death of Matilda a small portion
of his estates was restored to him by the Conqueror at the
dying request, it is said, of the Queen, whose belated repent-
ance was respected by William.

DOMESDAY BOOK.

It is interesting to notice that Gloucester was the birth-
place of the Domesday survey.   In a witan, or Grand Council,
held in Gloucester at Christmas, 1085, where we are told,
King William wore his crown, the idea of a general survey
was first debated.   A previous partial survey had been made
by Alfred the Great, but this was quite out of date.   And,
indeed, it was high time for an enquiry to be made.   The
country was in a deplorable state of confusion, starvation and
misery, owing chiefly to the ruthless destruction and spoliation by the Norman invaders, and by the heavy taxation
imposed by these pitiless taskmasters.

Writing of this Conference, in his valuable Analysis of
the Domesday Survey of Gloucestershire, the Rev. C. S. Taylor
says :—[1]

" No doubt all this was carefully considered at that Christmas Tide gathering (more than eight centuries ago) ; there were
giants in the art of Government in those days, and it is difficult
to know which we ought to admire most in the scheme which
they devised, whether the grandeur of its conception or the
magnificent powers of organisation which were displayed in
its fulfillment."

The Anglo-Saxon Chronicle tells us that " The King
sent his men all over England, into every Shire, and
caused them to ascertain how many hundred hides of land
it contained and what lands the King possessed therein,
what cattle there were in the several Counties, and how
much revenue he ought to receive yearly from each.   He
also caused them to write down how much land belonged
to his Archbishops, to his Bishops, his Abbots, and his
Earls, and, that I may be brief, what property every
inhabitant of all England possessed in land or in cattle
and how much money this was worth.   So very narrowly
did he cause the Survey to be made that there was not a
single hide nor a rood of land nor—it is shameful to relate

---

[1] Transactions of the B. & Gl. Archæolog, Soc., 1889.

what he thought it no shame to do—was there an ox, or a cow, or pig passed by that was not set down in the accounts, and. then all these writings were brought to him."

The Commissioners who visited Gloucestershire were Remigius Bishop of Lincoln, an able and powerful Prelate, Henry de Ferrieres and Walter Giffard both of whom fought at Hastings, and Adam fitz Herbert, Steward of the Royal Household, and right well they did the work entrusted to them.

The following extracts from Domesday Book relate to our two Manors. :—

The Manor of Minchinhampton included that of Rodborough and is stated to have contained 4940 acres, of which 3480 were cultivated, 1440 were wood, and 20 meadows. It was valued at £28. There were 32 " Villeins ; " 10 " Bordarii ; " and 10 " Servi " or Serfs, and one Priest is also mentioned. The distinction between these three classes of inhabitants is very interesting, but space will not allow us to say much on the subject. Roughly the Villeins were small landowners or farmers and freemen, the Bordarii or Cottars (from Latin *borda*, a cottage) were also free except that they had to do a certain amount of work for their lord. The lot of the Servi or Serfs was the hardest of all. They passed with the land from owner to owner, and had but little personal freedom, though from self-interest they were given a sufficiency of food to keep them in health. The most cruel incident of serfdom was the practice of selling them as slaves to places far distant from their homes, and, I regret to say that the citizens of Bristol were pre-eminent in this horrible traffic, and dreadful stories of the slave markets are quoted by Mr Taylor in his Analysis of the Domesday Survey. To his honour, be it said, St. Wulstan, Bishop of Worcester, came and lived in Bristol, preaching against the iniquities of the slave traffic. In the life of St. Wulstan it is said : " You might have seen with sorrow long ranks of young persons of both sexes and of the greatest beauty, tied with ropes, and daily exposed for sale." This traffic was illegal before the conquest and stringent laws against it were made by the Normans, but the trade was so profitable that it lingered on for many years, notwithstanding the heavy penalties imposed for its suppression.

It is recorded in Domesday Book that Brictric had a Park and enclosure for beasts of the chase at Old Sodbury and a " Hawke's Eyrey," or breeding place for hawks at Avening. The Manor of Avening is stated in Domesday to belong to the King, though it was probably given to the Abbey of Caen about the same time as that of Minchinhampton. It contained an area of 4320 acres, consisting of 2880 acres of cultivated land and 1440 of wood. There were 24 Villeins, 5 Bordarii and 30 Serfs, but no priest is mentioned. The value of the Manor is stated at £27—of course, equivalent to a much larger sum at the present day. Pennebaria (Pinbury) in the Parish of Duntisbourne Rouse, the Manor of which is held with that of Avening, is mentioned as belonging to the Abbey of Caen, and a smith (there are only two mentioned in Gloucestershire) is stated to have lived and held land on the estate of the Nuns of Caen. The Manor of Avening also included those of Aston and Lowesmore.

L'ABBAYE AUX DAMES, CAEN

CHAPTER V.

MINCHINHAMPTON AND AVENING UNDER THE NUNS OF CAEN

THE two Abbeys at Caen, L'Abbaye aux Hommes and L'Abbaye aux Dames were founded respectively by William and Matilda by way of penance for having married within the prohibited degrees of consanguinity in defiance of the Papal Council of Rheims. The relationship of William and Matilda was so remote that the Pope, Gregory VII., was probably influenced more by political than by moral considerations. At any rate, the needful dispensation was given by Pope Nicholas II. in 1059, and the two Abbeys were founded shortly after.

L'Abbaye aux Dames with which we are more nearly concerned, was founded in 1066, and was richly endowed by William and Matilda. The Nunnery was for ladies of noble birth, and the Abbess had the title of "Madame de Caen." The first Abbess was Cecily, the Conqueror's eldest daughter, and the annual revenue of the foundation amounted to 30,000 livres. The Abbey Church remains a noble and stately monument of the piety of the Founders, and perhaps we may draw a discreet veil over the methods by which it was endowed. The body of Matilda was buried in the centre of the Choir, but the Tomb was rifled in later years by the Huguenots, and her remains were scattered. They were, however, collected again and replaced in the Tomb, which was restored in 1819, and the original inscription was also replaced.

Hampton now became Minchinhampton, or Nun's Hampton, the prefix being an old word signifying a Nun.[1]

[1] "Minchin" represents the Middle English rendering of Anglo-Saxon Mynece, Mûnechene—. The Nuns' Hampton.—"Place-names of Gloucestershire," p. 109.

We do not hear much of the doings of the Nuns until some time after the Conquest. No doubt the two Churches of Minchinhampton and Avening were being built by them or by their influence. Avening Church, fortunately still retains much of the ancient Norman work, but from that of Hampton it has practically entirely disappeared. In the 13th century contentions arose between the Abbot of Cirencester on the one part and Beatrix Abbess of Caen on the other, which were ultimately settled on these terms :—

"The Abbess and Convent agreed for themselves and their successors, that the Bailiffs of the Abbot and Convent twice every year should come to the said manor to hold view of Frankpledge[1] in the Court of the Abbess and Convent, according as they have been accustomed, before the said contentions, to wit, about the feast of St. Martin and Hockday,[2] so that the view of St. Martin may be holden about the feast of St. Andrew and the view of Hockday about Pentecost, upon reasonable summons of the Abbot's bailiffs ; these bailiffs to be entertained with their horses and three servants in the Court of the Abbess, at her cost, as usual before these contentions. The Bedel also of the Hundred of Longtree, if he should come with the Abbot's bailiffs to Hampton at the said two days, to be honourably received and lodged ; the said bailiffs to receive also, for the use of their lords, from the Abbess and her successors, by the hand of her bailiff, every year, at each view, besides their hospitality, half a mark for all amerciaments, belonging to the said two days view of Frankpledge (pleas and attachments of the Crown, which could not be discussed in the Court of the Abbess, excepted) ; all fines and Amerciaments of the above two days to remain with the Abbess in consideration of the above half mark and hospitalities."

Fresh contentions of a similar nature, relating to the Manor of Avening, arose between the Abbot of Cirencester

---

[1] Frankpledge was a pledge or surety for freemen. The ancient custom of England for the preservation of public peace was that every free born man at the age of 16 (in some manors 14) years of age, clerics and knights, and their eldest sons excepted, should find security for his fidelity to the King or else be kept in prison ; whence it became a custom for neighbours to be bound for one another to see each man of their pledge forthcoming at all times to answer the transgression of any man absenting himself. This was called frankpledge, and the circuit commonly consisted of 10 or more households. This custom was strictly observed, and the Sheriffs in every county did from time to time take the oath of young men as they grew up and see that they combined in one dozen or other ; this branch of the Sheriff's duty was called "view of frankpledge."

[2] Hockday, or Hocktide, was an ancient holiday celebrated on the second Monday and Tuesday after Easter Sunday.

and the Abbess of Caen in the reign of Henry III., and these were settled in the following terms :—

"That if it happens in time to come that any of the men, tenants, resiants or bailiffs of the said Abbess and Convent of Hampton, Avening and Pinbury, with their appertenances in the hundreds of Cirencester and Longtree, shall be impleaded or inquieted, and on the part of the said Abbess, a Court of the Abbess may be asked for, according to the Common Law of the land, it may be granted ; and if it happens that any plaint, or want of petition in the Court of the Abbess in the hundreds aforesaid, may remain to be pleaded or determined, every of the said men, tenants, resiants or bailiffs of the said Manor, according to the Common Law of the land, to be amerced shall give for the amerciament only 6d. Also the steward of the Abbess for the time being before the said Abbot or his bailiffs, in the said hundred, to be impleaded or inquieted unless he may be called to warranty, or by personal transgression, or by precept, may not henceforward be compelled ; and if the steward *pro tempore*, at the time of the complaint or distress, shall be absent 20 miles from Cirencester, the Abbot and Convent of Cirencester grant for themselves, successors and bailiffs (as much as in them is), that it shall be lawful for the said steward *pro tempore*, to appoint his attorney by his letters patent in the said pleas and inquietudes and if in any manner he shall be amerced in the said Hundred, he shall give only 6d. for the said amerciament ; but the said Abbess by no means shall be compelled to come nor to answer in the said places, unless she shall be present, and when she shall come there and shall be amerced she shall give for the amerciament 6d."

Yet another dispute arose about the year 1170 between Thomond Abbot, Theoksbury (Tewkesbury) and the Nuns of Caen concerning the presentation to the Church of Avening. This contention was also amicably settled, the Nuns paying 20 marks to the Abbot. It is difficult to determine in these quarrels whether the Abbots were trying to bully the Nuns or whether the ladies were claiming more than was their due.

In the reign of Henry II. extensive grants were made to the English Manors of the Abbess of Caen of sac and soc (husbandry services) team and toll, the strange right of " infanguentheof "[1] and all dues in the borough and without.   In the 4th year of Richard I.   (1193) the Nuns appear to have been apprehensive of some encroachments on their rights in the two Manors, as we find this entry :—

> " Joan the Abbess and the Convent of the Holy Trinity of Caen paid one mark that it might be written in the Great Roll that William de Felstade claimed in the Court of our Lord the King, for the aforesaid Abbess and Convent, Hampton and Avening and Lowesmore and Eston (Aston) and Pendeby (Pinbury)."

Aston and Lowesmoor were, and still are, included in the Manor of Avening.

About this time there is an interesting letter addressed apparently to the Abbess on the destruction of the Abbey woods, showing that the theft of wood was practiced in very ancient times :—

> " The men of Avening say that its woods, namely, Wilverding and Hazelholt (Hazelwood) and Rallingsdene (? Rowden) and Westgrove are destroyed on their oaths to the value of sixty marks over and above the tenants' right for wood for their houses and hearths ; and when Simon took over the vills, 1000 swine could feed on them, but now only 500.   The men of Hantone say, on their oaths, that the destruction amounts to 60 marks, and that 2000 swine could be fed, but now not 1000—and this destruction was wrought by Charcoal burners[2] and by sales."

The custom followed by all the earlier Kings of England of taking into their own hands, during war, all the emoluments of manors held by alien foundations, creates some confusion, especially during the reigns of Edward III., Henry V., and others, when wars abroad were very frequent.   Thus Thomas, of Gloucester, Hugh Waterton and Catherine, his wife, and others held the two manors to farm during the wars.   Probably these were hard times for the tenants, as those who undertook

---

[1] Infanguentheof or more properly Infangthef or Infangtheof is compounded of three words, the preposition "in," the Anglo-Saxon words "fang" to catch and "Thef" or "theof" a thief.   It signifies the right of the Lord of the Manor to catch, judge and probably hang any thief taken within his fee.   The Abbess maintained a gallows for the two Manors, but I do not know where it was erected nor is there any record of a criminal suffering on it.

[2] Charcoal burning was practised up to quite recent times, and the writer remembers to have seen the huts and the fires on the Copse in the Parish of Avening.

to farm the rents of the Manors would naturally get as much as possible into their own pockets during their tenure, whereas the rule of the Nuns was far more indulgent. They were satisfied if the Firmarius, or bailiff, remitted a reasonable amount to his employers.

The Manor of Rodborough formed part of the Manor of Minchinhampton, and, in the reign of Edward I., it is described as a hamlet of Minchinhampton held by the Abbess of Caen. In the 33rd year of Edward III. it was held of the Abbess by an ancient family called de Rodberge or Rodbourge in soccage by 20s. per annum and the service of guarding her treasure from Minchinhampton to Southampton.

There is but little more to record as to the connection between our two Manors and the Convent of Caen, yet we get occasional glimpses which seem to show that they kept in close touch with their English possessions. The following are extracts from the " Memoires de la Société des Antiquaires de Normandie : "—

" Julienne Abbesse de Sainte Trinité de Caen fait un accord en 1237, avec Guilleaume Mael de Hampton au sujet de diverses redevances qu'elle réclamait sur les terres qu'il possédait en Angleterre.

" Roger de Salinges, recteur de l'église de Hampton en Angleterre consent à faire un échange de terre avec l'Abbaye de Sainte Trinité contre un acre de terre situé dans le grand champ de Hampton."

Except for the interruptions mentioned above, the two Manors remained in the possession of the Nuns of Caen till the year 1415, when an Act of Parliament was passed permanently confiscating for the use of the King all buildings and endowments belonging to foreign ecclesiastical foundations, and thus the Nuns ceased to have any further interest in their Gloucestershire possessions, which they had held for no less than 333 years. There was some reason for this confiscation, as it was a common practice for the owners of the Alien foundations to cause their bailiffs to collect all the money they could raise and send it to the foreign head Houses, where it could be used by the King's enemies during war. Though confiscated for the King's use the endowments were mostly given to existing ecclesiastical foundations or used for building and endowing new ones.

In the year 1213 Minchinhampton became a town, the Abbess of Caen having in that year purchased the privilege of a weekly Market and two Fairs, which were held, according to the modern calendar, on Trinity Monday and the 29th of October, and this right was subsequently confirmed to Lord Windsor by Queen Elizabeth. Hampton Fair was regularly held until recent times, and the writer remembers often to have seen the cattle and horses in the streets. Fresh regulations were made in 1825, but both Markets and Fairs have now disappeared, owing to the competition of the larger Markets served by the Railways, and giving greater facilities both to buyers and sellers. But at least they have a remarkable record, having existed for more than six and a half centuries, and having brought considerable prosperity to the town and neighbourhood during that long period.

CHAPTER VI.

THE TWO MANORS UNDER THE NUNS OF SYON

OUR two manors now passed, with many others, into the possession of the great Bridgettine foundation of Syon Abbey, though, as was commonly the case with the confiscated endowments, they were subject to a grant for lives by the King before becoming the absolute property of the foundations to which they had been allotted. Thus in the case of the manors of Minchinhampton and Avening, William de la Pole, Earl of Suffolk, and Alice, his wife, were their owners for life, and the Abbey did not come into full possession of them till the reign of Henry VI.

Before sailing on his expedition to France, which ended so gloriously with the victory of Agincourt, Henry V., by his first will, dated July 24, 1415, bequeathed to the foundation 1,000 marks in gold for the building of their house, the value of the site of which is stated at £1 13s 4d p. ann. The foundation stone of Syon Abbey was laid by Henry himself on his return from France, in the presence of Richard Clifford, Bishop of London, and a charter dated February 22, 1415, according to the calendar then in use,[1] was also granted to the community. This Charter decrees that it shall be founded " under the name of S. Saviour and S. Bridget of the order of S. Augustine, and that it shall be so called throughout all succeeding ages." By the same charter the Bridgettines of Syon are bound " to celebrate Divine Service for ever for our healthful estate while we live and for our soul when we have departed this life, and for the souls of our most dear lord and father, Henry, late King of England, and Mary his late wife, our most dear mother."

[1] According to the old calendar the year began on March 25th.

The monastery was most liberally endowed by its Royal Founder, and soon attained to great wealth and influence, many privileges being granted to it. Amongst others, is a quaint bequest of " four tuns of wine of Gascony to be received yearly from the wines of us and of our heirs in the port of the city of London, by the hands of our Chief Butler, at the feast of S. Martin in winter." In the year 1432, eighteen years after its foundation, Henry VI. granted permission to the Abbess and Convent of Syon to remove to a more spacious edifice which they had built on their demesne in the parish of Isleworth. The new monastery was built of stone brought from Caen, whether from sentiment or whether it was the best that could be obtained, does not appear. It was brought regularly by the ship " Mary of Caen," of 80 tons, which was given safe conduct by land, sea, and river in all parts inland and foreign subject to the King's dominion.

The nuns, as already mentioned, were of the order of S. Saviour and S. Bridget, and went by the name of Bridgettines. S. Bridget was born in 1302 of wealthy and influential parents, and, having been compelled at an early age to marry Ulf, Prince of Nericia, she became the mother of eight children, one of whom was also canonised under the name of S. Catherine of Sweden. Bridget's saintly and charitable life soon made her known far and wide over the north of Europe, and she also gained great religious influence over her husband. They eventually, however, separated by mutual consent, he becoming a monk in the Cistercian Abbey of Alvastra, in East Gothland, where he died in 1344.

S. Bridget was now free to undertake the great work of founding the new order to which she devoted the remaining years of her life. She died in Rome, July 23, 1372, at the age of 71, and was canonised eighteen years after her death by Pope Boniface IX. (Tomacelli). In founding the new Order, S. Bridget was greatly aided by her daughter, S. Catherine, and the community soon attained to a high position and became famous throughout the whole of the north of Europe. It was visited by Philippa, sister of Henry V., immediately after her marriage to Eric, King of Norway, Sweden and Denmark, in 1406. Amongst others in her train when she made this visit was Henry third Lord Fitzhugh, Lord of the Bedchamber to Henry V., who, becoming greatly impressed with the sanctity of the Order, determined to introduce it into England. He accordingly offered to settle his manor of Hinton, near Cambridge, on a colony of the order, if one were sent over, and, on its establishment in its new home, he supported it most generously from his private purse, and at his death left £20 a year for its maintenance.[1]

The Bridgettine foundations consisted of 85 persons answering to our Saviour's 13 apostles, S. Paul included, and 72 disciples ; they were represented by 60 nuns or sisters, whereof one was Lady Abbess, 13 priests, one of whom was to preside over the men as Confessor General, four deacons, representing the 4 Doctors of the Church (Ambrose, Augustine, Jerome, and Gregory), four lay sisters as kitchen maids for the nuns, and four lay brothers for similar services to the monks and to be generally useful about the place. The nuns and monks lived in separate courts divided by the Abbey Church, which was common to both, the nuns during the services being behind a grille in such a position that they could see the High Altar. The monks were to sing the Divine Office, and the nuns the Office of our Lady, according to the Bridgettine rite. The men were to sing their part first and the sisters after they had finished. They had also to rise during the night for Matins and Lauds. The rule of S. Bridget was a severe one, additional fasts, besides the ordinary ones ordained by the Church, being enjoined. The bedding was of straw, but the bolster and pillow might be covered with linen, and two blankets were also allowed. The dress for the nuns, as also for the Abbess, was of grey serge, " which must not be gathered or pleated, but cut straight and plain—all for profit and nothing for vanity." Over the black veiled whimple, or coif, there is a distinctive coronal of white linen strips in the form of a cross with 5 red cloth patches to typify the Crown of Thorns and the Five Wounds, and a grey mantle is also worn. The lay sisters wore a white maltese cross with 5 red circles on the left shoulder of the mantle, and the monks also wore a cross on their habits over the heart. Each nun wears a signet ring, which is a facsimile of that worn by S. Bridget after her husband's death. The present Lady Abbess is the 59th in succession, and their Office is exactly identical, both in words and in chant, with that used by their predecessors at

[1] It is interesting to note that Sir Maurice de Berkeley, of Beverston Castle, married Laura, daughter of this same Lord Fitzhugh, and another Sir Maurice, son of the above, held the manor of Cheltenham on lease from the nuns of Syon.

Isleworth. The Abbess was Principal over both the men and
the women, and had the management of the revenues derived
from the endowments and from the industry of the nuns.
Silence was strictly enjoined at meals and at other times
except during certain specified hours. The table of signs to
be used during these periods of silence is very quaint. Two
examples will suffice : " Fyshe—wagge thy hand displaid
sidelings in manner of a fissh taill." " Mustard—hold thy
nose in the upper part of thy right fist and rubbe it."

In the year 1426, the first stone of a new Monastery
Church was laid by John, Duke of Bedford, Regent during
the minority of Henry VI., in the presence of the Bishops of
London and Winchester. In 1444, King Henry granted to
the Abbess in frankalmoign,[1] or tenure by Divine Service,
the manor of Minchinhampton, parcel of the possession of the
alien monastery of Caen. The nuns did not come immediately
into the income of their property, and this seems to have been
their first entry into full possession of their estates.

During the short period in which Henry VI was restored
to the throne, the nuns, apprehensive, no doubt, that their
possessions might not be safeguarded in these troublous times,
petitioned for confirmation of their rights, and, during the
year 1492, a complete survey of all their estates and possessions was made. This survey disclosed the fact that they
owned no less than 40 manors and the tithes of 30 parishes,
besides many other possessions, the whole amounting to
£2,000 p. ann., a very large sum in those days. In this survey
we come across the mention for the first time of the manor of
Avening, though it presumably came into their possession at
the same time as the manor of Minchinhampton. Avening
is stated to be worth £29 1s 4½d p. ann., and Minchinhampton,
included in the same survey, is valued at £91 1s 2½d p. ann.
In yet another survey, made just before the dissolution of the
monasteries, mention is made of lands and tenements lately
of the Lady Alicia Hampton amounting to £9 4s 5d.

Nunneries were often places of refuge for females in time
of war, and at the time of the Norman Conquest, many Saxon
women took the black veil of nuns as a safeguard from the
licentiousness of the conquerors. Afterwards, when they

[1] "They which hold in frankalmoign are bound of right before God to make orisons, prayers and
other Divine services for the soul of the grantor." Ency. Britt.

wished to return to society, it was ordered that those who had taken refuge for this reason and did not wish to remain as nuns should be absolved from their vows and allowed to leave. Convents were also places of education for young women, many of them daughters of the nobility, up to the time of their dissolution.

The time had now come when all monastic institutions were suppressed and despoiled of their possessions, and thus the long connection between our two manors and the Church, which had existed for 500 years, ceased, and they passed from ecclesiastical into secular hands. In the year 1534, Henry VIII. having thrown off the papal authority, caused a general valuation and visitation of ecclesiastical foundations to be made by the notorious Thomas Cromwell, who was appointed Vicar General and vice-regent of the King. The Abbey of Syon, amongst others, was surrendered to the King's Commissioners in 1539. This was during the term of office, as Abbess, of Agnes Jordan, who was elected in 1531, and had practically spent her whole life at Syon, as the name occurs as a sister in 1518. It must have been a sad day indeed when the Abbess and the community looked their last on the home they had loved so well and where all their religious life had been passed. Pensions for life were given to the nuns and the monks who took the oath acknowledging Henry as Head of the Church. Some of the monks, but very few of the nuns, conformed and accepted the pensions, which, except in the case of the Abbess, did not err on the side of generosity, as the full sisters received £6 yearly, and the lay sisters £2 13s 4d. Many of the monks who refused to conform were hanged, drawn and quartered, and amongst others, " the Angel of Syon," Richard Reynolds, who was drawn to Tyburn on a hurdle, and there suffered the barbarous penalty with all its horrible details. Part of the remains were placed on a pillar of the gateway of old Syon Abbey, and when they finally left England, the nuns actually carried the cumbrous capital through all their wanderings, and it is now preserved at Syon Abbey, at Chudleigh.

The Abbess, Agnes Jordan, was one of those who had not the strength of mind to remain stedfast, but eventually conformed and received the highest scale pension of £200 a year as a reward for her conformity. But perhaps it is not quite fair to blame overmuch those who had not the strength to resist in this terrible time of persecution and destruction of all Catholic institutions ; and it is a greater wonder that so many remained stedfast than that a few found the trial too great to bear.

Whatever may be said against the monasteries at the time of the Reformation— and some was true, and much was exaggerated—they had at least served a useful purpose in their day.   They had kept alive learning and literature which, but for them, would not have survived the wars and chaos of the Middle Ages, and they fostered religion and respect for law.   They were pre-eminent in charity, and, as we have seen, nunneries protected women who, but for them, would have passed their lives in misery and dishonour.   No doubt some of the monasteries were not all they should have been, and perhaps they had to a great extent outlived their usefulness ; yet we must remember that it was necessary for Henry VIII. and his aiders and abettors to find or invent causes of offence in the monasteries to justify the wholesale spoliation of their possessions.   But the history of the Reformation belongs to the history of England, and we must pass on to events more immediately relating to our two manors.

It may not be uninteresting to add the names of the Abbesses of Syon from its foundation to the time of its final suppression in England :—

1415	Matilda Newton	1456	Dorothy Graham
1428	Joan North	1461	Elizabeth Gibbes
1433	Matilda Huxton	1518	Constantia Browne
1447	Margaret Ashby	1531	Agnes Jordan
1456	Bridget Walgrave	1557	Catherine Palmer
1456	Elisabeth Muston	1557	Clementina Tresham

The last two were probably appointed by Queen Mary during the short reinstatement of the nuns.

The subsequent history of the Bridgettine nuns of Syon is most interesting.   On August 1st, 1557, in the last year of the reign of Queen Mary, the nuns who had fled to the Bridgettine convent at Termonde, in Flanders, were recalled to England by Philip and Mary, on the petition of Cardinal Pole, who had visited them in their foreign home.   Their former convent was restored to them, but it was shorn of its grandeur, and the endowments were very different to those which they had formerly possessed. The Abbess who succeeded Agnes Jordan, and who had brought back the remnant of the community to England, was Catherine Palmer, who died soon after their return, and it is interesting to notice that the Prioress was Margaret Windsor, the sister of Lord Windsor, who now owned the two manors of Minchinhampton and Avening. Every effort was made by the brother to induce his sister to conform, but she remained stedfast and went into exile, subsequently returning with the rest on their short restoration. At the time of the dissolution the seal of the monastery was in the custody of sister Agnes Smyth, who is described as a " sturdy dame and wilful." She absolutely refused to give up the seal, which was taken away by the nuns, and is now, I believe, preserved at Chudleigh.

The restoration of the community to their former home was very short-lived, as in the following year the death of Mary and the accession of Elizabeth compelled the nuns once more to flee to Termonde. Here they remained four years and in 1563 the Spanish Regent placed at their disposal a disused monastery on the Zuyder Zee, in a damp and unhealthy situation. After a time, sickness compelled them to leave these surroundings, and, through the generosity of an exiled Catholic, they were established in a house at Mechlin. After remaining at this home for seven years they had again to escape from Lutheran hostility owing to the Netherlands revolt, and it is pleasant to be able to record that in their dire extremity, after being plundered of all their possessions, they were rescued by some English Protestant officers serving in the army of the Prince of Orange, who, at the risk of their lives, escorted their countrywomen to Antwerp.

On several occasions they sent members of the community to solicit alms, but they received only persecution and imprisonment instead of the help they went to seek. Space will not allow us to follow their further wanderings, how they fled to Rouen, suffering starvation, poverty and misery ; how these dauntless women under their Confessor Father Foster sailed down the Seine on Good Friday, 1594, and how, after suffering further imprisonment and robbery, they embarked on board a ship bound to Lisbon, and, narrowly escaping capture by pirates on several occasions, they eventually reached

the mouth of the Tagus on May 20, 1594. Thus, after 37 years
of dangers, privations and wandering, they found rest at last.
Novices began to arrive from England, the convent continuing
to be, as it has always been, a purely English community.
They were not, however, to escape without further misfortunes.
On May 24, 1628, Father Foster, who had been their guide and
Confessor through all their wanderings, died, to their great
grief ; and in the year 1651 their convent was destroyed by
fire, and they were once more homeless. Through the generosity of the King of Portugal the buildings were restored, but
the terrible earthquake of 1755 again laid it in ruins. By
earnest appeals to English Catholics, they were enabled
to re-build their convent, where they remained in peace
till 1809. The outbreak of the Peninsular War caused further
misfortune to the nuns, their convent being taken by Wel-
lington's troops as a hospital for the wounded. Nine of the
sisters, headed by the frightened Abbess, Mary Theresa Hal-
ford, decided to return to England, and, unfortunately, they
took with them most of the valuables belonging to the order,
amongst them being the famous Syon Cope, one of the most
beautiful specimens of ancient needlework in existence. Misfortune dogged the steps of this party, and they eventually
died out. But they had been obliged to part with all their
valuables to save themselves from starvation, and their last
possession, the cope, was given to the Earl of Shrewsbury, who
had generously come to their rescue. On the death of Lord
Shrewsbury, the cope, after passing through other hands, was
finally purchased for the nation, and is now in the South
Kensington Museum.[1]

Meanwhile, the minority left at Lisbon were accommodated
for a time at an Irish Dominican convent, and, on the restoration of peace, they returned to their old home. Finally, owing
to the anti-religious laws in Portugal, which forbade them to
receive novices, the remaining sisters, eleven in number, returned to England in 1861, and, after living for some years at
Spettisbury in Dorset, they found a resting place at last at
Chudleigh, in S. Devon, where, by the benefactions of English
Catholics, the house in which they now reside was built, and
also a beautiful church adjacent to it. Thus, this most

---

[1] The Syon Cope was purchased for the Museum in 1864. It is late 13th. century work and is
in excellent preservation. Its main features are scenes from the life of Christ and the Virgin, and
figures of St. Michael, and other Angels with six wings standing on wheels, and also figures of the
Apostles.

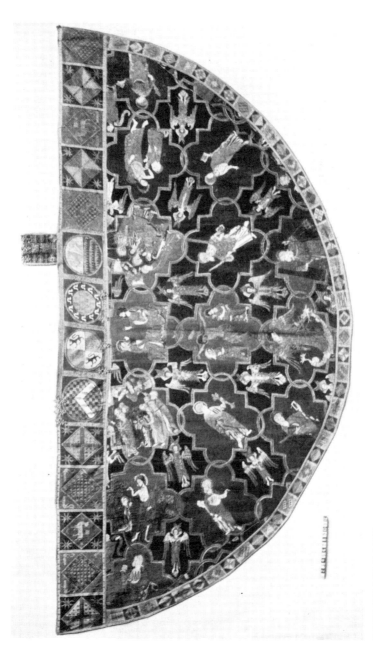

THE SYON COPE

interesting Order, the only pre-Reformation community in England, and which has existed for 500 years, has found peace at last, and all who admire courage, constancy and devotion will wish them a long and prosperous future.

After the final confiscation of all monastic endowments, the two manors, together with the advowsons of the livings, after being held for a few years by the King, were, in 1543, granted by him to Andrew, 1st Baron Windsor (so created Nov. 3rd, 1529), in exchange for the Manor of Stanwell, in Middlesex. There was a payment to the Exchequer of £2,197 5s 8d, and a reserved rent of £8 14s 0d for Minchinhampton, and £2 8s 3d for Avening, including Aston and Losemoor. The Manor of Pinbury Park, under the name of Pinbourne, was also transferred to Lord Windsor at the same time. It is strange with regard to the latter Manor, that though it was sold to Sir Henry Poole, of Sapperton, in 1600, it still belongs to the Manor of Avening, and fee farm rent in respect of it is paid by the Lord of that Manor to the present day.

After remaining in the Windsor family for several generations, the Manor passed on the death of Thomas Lord Windsor in 1642 to his nephew, Thomas Hickman. The last Lord Windsor is said to have been " seized of the Manor of Minchinhampton, Aveninge, Loysemore, Ashton, Redborough, Noilsworth, Strowed, and 30 messuages, 30 tofts, 6 water mills, 6 dovecots, 30 gardens, 1,000 acres of land, 200 of mead, 1,000 of pasture, 2,000 of wood, 300 of common, held of the King by knight's service." Notwithstanding these large possessions he seems to have left heavy debts behind him, and the trustees of Thomas Hickman, who was a minor, in order to liquidate these, were forced in the year 1651 to sell the two Manors of Avening and Minchinhampton, with the advowsons and other appertenances, to Samuel Sheppard.

By the kindness of Mr F. A. Hyett, of Painswick House, I am able to give an account of the connection of his ancestors with the Manor of Nailsworth, which seems to have been a separate Manor, though within the parish of Avening :—

James Hyett, of Lydney, who was Constable of St. Briavels Castle in 1471, and was in the latter year collector of tenths and land tax, is described in the Polls Receipt

Roll (14 Edw. IV.) as having lately been the owner of the Manor of Nailsworth. He had recently made it over to his son Roger, who died during his father's lifetime, Oct. 20th, 1478. At the "inquistiones post mortem," held respecting Roger's property, it was found that he held a lease of the Manor of Naylesworth from the Monastery of S. Saviour of Zion, and that his brother Thomas, who was then 14 years old, was his heir. The Manor descended to Thomas and was his property until his death on Feb. 20th, 1543. He left a son, James, to whom the lease of the Manor of Nailsworth passed. James had a son, Charles, and a grandson, Richard, who joined together in selling their interest in the Manor of Nailsworth and three messuages in Naylesworth and Minchinhampton to Henry Lord Windsor, for the sum of £200 (Feet of Fines 43 and 44 Elizabeth).

These early ancestors of Mr Hyett would have had cause to feel proud indeed if they could have foreseen the literary talent, and the immense amount of public work, voluntarily and gratuitously undertaken by their descendant, in the 20th Century, and the conspicuous ability with which this work is carried out.

The interests of the Hyetts in the Manor of Nailsworth was, as was frequently the case in monastic Manors, only that of lessees, and it formed part of the possession of Syon Abbey, seized by Henry VIII. and given, as we have mentioned above, to Andrew Lord Windsor.

This leasing of Manors for a term of years or for lives, was a very common practice, especially in the case of Manors belonging to monastic foundations in out-of-the-way parts of the country, where the owners were very much in the hands of their "Firmarius," or bailiff. Many of these bailiffs rose to great power and opulence—by what means we can only conjecture.

There is an interesting account of a Court Leet held on March 12th, 1507, by Dame Alice Hampton, who is described as a lady of "approved chastity," either on behalf of the Abbess of Syon or, more probably, because she had leased the manorial rights from the Foundation which would revert again to the Abbess at her death.

CHAPTER VII.

THE SHEPPARD FAMILY

THE Sheppard Family played so large a part in the history of Minchinhampton and Avening for nearly 200 years that it is necessary to refer somewhat at length to their story. A great part of the following facts are taken from an article which the writer contributed to *Gloucestershire Notes and Queries* about the year 1884, in answer to an enquiry from America as to the history of one branch of the family seated at Colesborne, in this County.

The Sheppards were descended from a family seated at Peasmarch, in Sussex, and Battersea, near London. They first appear in Gloucestershire at Horsley, where the following notices occur :—

Baptisms—

Elizabeth, daughter of William Sheppard,			June 22,	1622
Sarah do.	do.	do.	June 27,	1624
Samuel, son of	do.	do.	March 26,	1627
Anne, daughter of	do.	do.		1628
Dorothy do.	do.	do.		1637

Marriages—

Samuel Sheppard and Elizabeth ———		1627
Joseph Clifford and Mary Sheppard ..	August 14,	1638
John Mills and Judith Sheppard ..	September 21,	1654

Burial—

Philip Sheppard	September 20,	1623

This Philip Sheppard left three sons, William of Hempstead, John of Tetbury, and Samuel of Minchinhampton, and one daughter Rebecca, wife of Charles Hillar (Hillier), of

PEDIGREE OF SHEPPARD OF MINCHINHAMPTON AND AVENING

PHILIP SHEPPARD OF HORSLEY, OB. 1623 = Isabel, daughter of George North of Buckington, c. Wilts

SAMUEL SHEPPARD (1st.) purchased Minchinhampton and Avening Manors from Trustees of Lord Windsor in 1651. Ob. Mar. 11, 1672, ætat 70.
= 1st. Elizabeth, daughter of Sir Gamaliel Capel of Rookwood Hall, Essex. Ob. 1663
2nd. Frances, daughter of Francis Lord Seymour of Trowbridge and relict of William Ducie Lord Downe. Ob. s. p.

PHILIP SHEPPARD (2nd) Justice of the Peace for Gloucestershire and Barrister-at-law of the Middle Temple. Ob. 1713, ætat 82.
= Anne, daughter and heiress of Thos. Webb of Wallbridge, Stroud. Ob. 1734, ætat 73

SAMUEL SHEPPARD (2nd.) Ob. Aug. 29th. 1724, ætat 63
= Anne, daughter of Edward Darell of Rockhampton, Surrey. Ob. Aug. 29, 1749, ætat 59.

SAMUEL SHEPPARD (3rd) High Sheriff of Gloucestershire 1730. Ob. Dec. 20, 1749, ætat 53
= Mary, daughter of Thos. Knight of Eastington. Ob. May 11, 1753, ætat 49.

PHILIP SHEPPARD (3rd) Rector of Minchinhampton and Avening. Ob. Dec. 15, 1768, ætat 73, s. p.

SAMUEL SHEPPARD (4th) Ob. Oct. 29. 1770, ætat 51
= Jane, daughter of Thos. Horwood of Halton, Oxon. Ob. 1799, ætat 74.

EDWARD SHEPPARD of Gatcombe Park, Ob. June 12, 1803, ætat 78.
= Sarah, daughter of Chas. Cox of Kemble Park, Glos. Ob. May 5, 1789, ætat 59.

PHILIP SHEPPARD (4th) last owner of Gatcombe and of the Manors of Minchinhampton and Avening, died 1838.
= Elizabeth, daughter of Rev. Charles Lee of Bristol.

Philip Sheppard left two sons Edward and Philip Charles. The latter married Mary, only daughter of Osborne Markham by his first wife, Mary, daughter of Thomas, first Marquis of Bath. He died July, 1878, having had fourteen children, of which eleven were living in 1883. His two elder sons are married and have large families.

Horsley. William was married four times and John thrice, but I know nothing of their descendants. The third son, Samuel, purchased the Manors of Minchinhampton and Avening from the trustees of Lord Windsor in 1651, though I think there had been some previous transactions between Lord Windsor and Samuel's father. Samuel married Isabel, daughter of George North, of Buckington, Co. Wilts. (a sister of one of his brother William's wives), and died March 11th, 1672. The issue of this marriage was two sons and two daughters. Samuel, the elder son, died young, and Philip, a Justice of the Peace for the County of Gloucester and barrister at law, inherited his father's estates. Atkyns says of him, " Philip Sheppard is the present Lord of the Manor of Minchinhampton and keeps a Court Leet. He has a large house near the Church and a spacious grove of high trees in a park adjoining to it, which is seen at a great distance. He hath a very large estate in this and other parishes within this county." Abel Wantner, writing about 1710, says : " Just behind Squire Sheppard's most pleasant habitation groweth one of the finest groves of pine-like ash and beechen trees in all ye County ; County do I say, nay, in all ye Kingdom." Philip died in 1713, aged 82, and is buried at Minchinhampton. By his first wife he had two sons and two daughters. Samuel, the elder, succeeded to the Hampton and Avening estates, and Philip to Colesbourne, where he became the ancestor of the Colesbourne branch of the family.

Samuel Sheppard married Ann, only daughter and heiress of Thomas Webb, of Wallbridge, near Stroud (who died in 1734, aged 70, and was buried at Minchinhampton), by whom he had six sons and three daughters. This lady probably brought a considerable fortune to her husband, as in the next generation the family occupied an important position in the county. Three of the sons and one daughter died unmarried. William, the sixth son, is described as of " Hackney, Middlesex, Blackwell Hall Factor," from which we may infer that he was a wholesale cloth merchant.

Samuel, the eldest brother, inherited the family estates, and was a Justice of the Peace and High Sheriff in 1730. He married Anne, daughter of Edward Darell, of Rockhampton, Surrey, who died on August 29th, 1749, aged 58. Her husband did not long survive her, as he died on December 20th in the same year. On his tombstone in Minchinhampton Churchyard

is this epitaph, and if he possessed all the virtues ascribed to
him, he must indeed have been a remarkable man :—

IN MEMORY OF

SAMUEL SHEPPARD ESQUIRE

A gentleman of unblemished integrity, unaffected piety
And truly primitive simplicity of manners,
Affable and courteous in his behaviour,
Easy and instructive in his conversation,
Just and upright in all his dealings,
Without partiality, without hypocrisy,
His charity was as free from ostentation
As his nature from disguise.
In all social offices he remarkably excelled ;
An eminent example of conjugal affection,
A tender parent, a kind master, a sincere friend.
Thus adorned with an uncommon sanctity of morals,
He sustained the miseries of human life with
Christian fortitude,
His conscience not reproaching him
With the omission of any duty to God or man.
He was patient in his death,
And his hope was full of immortality.
He died December the 20th, 1749,
In the 63rd year of his age.

Samuel, the fourth of the name, succeeded to the estates,
but, as he left no male issue, they devolved on his younger
brother Edward on his death in 1770. The family had now
risen to considerable importance, and the estates, as shown by
rent rolls and accounts, had greatly increased in value.
Edward, therefore, on coming into possession of the property,
appears to have considered the old home at Minchinhampton
to be no longer adequate to the dignity to which the family
had attained ; and he accordingly built a new house at Gatcombe, in a beautiful situation about a mile from Minchinhampton, the residence of Major (now Lt. Col.) Ricardo.
The House, described by Fosbrooke as " The elegant modern
seat of the Sheppard family," is a fine mansion with a very
good front elevation. The plaster work inside the house is
in the Adams style, and all the details are extremely well carried
out. One would like to know the name of the architect who
designed it, but I have not been able to find any record on

this point. I do not know how long a time was employed in the building of the Mansion, nor the amount which it cost, but it must have involved Edward Sheppard in considerable expense, and at his death, June 12, 1803, at the age of 78, the property was already mortgaged.

The next heir and last owner of the old Sheppard Estates was Philip, only son of Edward. He was born in 1766, and was, consequently, about 37 years old when his father died. He is described as having been an easy-going, good-natured man, very extravagant, and with a great taste for sport and expensive amusements. He raised a troop of Yeomanry in 1795, the equipment and maintenance of which cost him a large amount of money. He also kept a pack of fox hounds at Gatcombe, which were not looked on with much favour by his father, if we may judge from an entry in a pocket-book of 1790 :—" Phil talked of giving up ye hounds ; I hope he may continue in yt resolution." There is also, in the same pocket-book, an account of a great run which Phil had with his hounds from Calcot Barn.

On his accession to the property, efforts were made to free it from encumbrances by the sale of the advowsons of the rectories of Minchinhampton and Avening. But the sums realized fell far short of the amount required, and the circumstances of the poor squire went from bad to worse. He was strongly urged to economise and live quietly for a few years, so as to give the estate time to recover. But it was not in his nature to do this, and he continued his career of extravagance. Household bills began to fall in arrear and creditors pressed for money. He endeavoured to stave off ruin by mortgaging the estates more deeply and selling off parts of the property. I have heard stories from his steward Baldwin, who lived in Minchinhampton to a great age, of the shifts to which he and the squire were put to raise ready money, and of the long consultations they often held far into the night to devise ways and means of tiding over the more pressing difficulties, At this time the old home of the family at Hampton was sold, and was subsequently pulled down, as we shall see later on.

The crash came at last, and in 1812 the manor of Avening, with most of the property in that parish, was sold to William Playne, of Longfords, who had already advanced considerable sums of money, and in 1814 Mr David Ricardo bought the

manor of Hampton with all the remaining property in that
parish.

Philip Sheppard soon afterwards went to live at Dun-
querque, in France, out of the reach of his creditors. The
writer's grandfather helped him over some of his difficulties,
and they corresponded till Philip Sheppard's death in London,
in December, 1838. He left two sons, Edward and Philip
Charles. Edward left no descendants, but the family was
continued by Philip Charles, and amongst the many descendants now living is Mr Thomas Falconer, whom we have
already mentioned, and who is the great grandson of Philip
Sheppard, the last owner of Gatcombe. The arms of the
Sheppard family were, Ermine on a chief sable three battle
axes argent.

There is a curious story of another very extravagant inhabitant of Minchinhampton, who flashed like a meteor across
the quiet life of the town, and disappeared and was heard of
no more.

Somewhere about the year 1824, or 1825, William Whitehead appears on the scene. He came into a large fortune of
over £100,000, inherited from his father, who was a Merchant
in London.

William Playne was one of the two official assignees in
Whitehead's bankruptcy, and hence it is that I have very
voluminous bundles of papers connected with the estate. The
balance sheets disclose an extraordinary state of affairs.
Whitehead seems to have bought property all over this part
of the county in the most reckless manner. His method of
acquiring these properties was immediately on purchase to
mortgage them for as much as he could raise. The
rate of interest, with this security, was 5%—a very moderate
rate at that time. The variety of property he bought was
remarkable, and below are a few of the most noteworthy :—

Hyde Farm, subsequently sold by the assignees
    to Mr David Ricardo £14,500
The Park, Westfield, the Shard, and sundry
    buildings and cottages £26,696
Other Cottages and lands in Minchinhampton £11,178
Lodgemore Mills, with steam engine, &c., &c.
    let to Nathaniel Marling at £1,800 p. ann. £27,000

and many other large amounts in other parts of the county
at Painswick, Nailsworth, etc.

THE REV. PHILIP SHEPPARD

Whitehead pulled down the old home of the Sheppards near the Church, and made a large walled garden, which still exists, within the grounds, and greatly enlarged the stables and outbuildings. He laid the foundation of a very large house, which was to be called " Minchinhampton Abbey," but it never rose beyond the foundation, still remaining under the present Schools, which were built on the site. All this might not have brought him to ruin had his life and character been better. In the first balance sheet, on paper at any rate, he was solvent, though in all probability the assets did not realize the amount at which they were valued. But he was reckless and extravagant to the last degree, keeping the lowest company, racing and gambling and spending money in the wildest manner. It is remarkable that all through the correspondence he is only once mentioned as being in Hampton, and then on the occasion of some drunken debauch. There are petitions from debtors' prisons of others whom he brought to ruin, but I do not know what ultimately became of him or where he died after his wasted life. Very probably, like many others, he fled the country to avoid being arrested. In a conversation with Philip Sheppard, towards the end of his life, my grandfather told him Whitehead's story, and how he got rid of £100,000 in little more than 13 months. " What," said Philip Sheppard, " Get rid of £100,000 in 13 months ! What a clever fellow he must have been ! It took me 13 years to get rid of about the same amount ! "

Whilst on the subject of the Sheppard family we must go back to the story of one member who no doubt was a well-known character in the neighbourhood in his day.

The Rev. Philip Sheppard was born in 1695, and became Rector of Minchinhampton, at the age of 25, in 1720, and of Avening in 1728. Both rectories were valuable benefices, and he occupied them till his death in 1768, having been rector of Minchinhampton for no less than 49 years, as is recorded on a tablet to his memory in the Chancel of Hampton Church. The illustration is from a portrait in the writer's possession. He married a Miss Knight, of Eastington, who died May 11, 1735, aged 49, and is buried at Minchinhampton. They had no children, but this lady probably brought some fortune to her husband, as land at Eastington is mentioned in his will. He built the present rectory house, which was

extensively altered by the Rev. E. C. Oldfield. I remember
the old house with narrow Georgian sash windows. He also
planted the avenue of limes which lead up to it, and which
are now very fine trees and a conspicuous landmark.

The advowsons and presentation to the livings belonged
to Philip Sheppard's nephew, Edward, under a settlement
made by his father. Perhaps he was intended for the Church,
but he never took orders. In the year 1765, Edward Sheppard,
in consequence of the state of his uncle's health, was anxious
to sell the next presentation to the livings of Minchinhampton
and Avening, and the following is a letter from Mr Edmund
Clutterbuck, the family solicitor, who lived at Hyde, dated
21st September, 1765 :—

" I cannot procure you an exact acct. how the yearly
income is made out by the present incumbent, who is
Mr Edward Sheppard's uncle, having kept no account
thereof. But the livings are generally esteemed to be
£700 p. ann., though 'tis well known that the present
Incumbent, who is an easy gent., does not make the most
of them. Mr Sheppard does not chuse to abate anything of £3,000, and he thinks that sum, considering the
age and infirmity of his Uncle (who is upwards up of 70
and who had some time ago a Stroke of the Palsy, by which
he has been lame ever since) is much under the value.
I assure you, Sir, I cannot think the present Incumbent's
life worth more than 4 or 5 years' purchase, indeed I
should not chuse to purchase his life at that, as being
unable to do duty himself, he keeps three curates, to
two of whom he gives £40 p. ann. and to the other £30.
The Parsonage House at Hampton, where the present
Incumbent lives, was new built by him, and is as pleasant
and convenient a dwelling as most in Gloucestershire."

This letter was written to a certain John Heaton, of
Threadneedle Street, London, who ultimately bought the two
livings for £2,900. Mr Clutterbuck's surmise was right, for
the old Rector lived only four years after the date of this
transaction. The Rev. Robert Salusbury Heaton was probably
the son of John Heaton, the purchaser of the living. He was
presented by Thomas Griffin and Edmund Clutterbuck, who
were Trustees and held the purchase money until the death
of Philip. The Rev. R. S. Heaton did not hold the living long,
as he died in 1774.

CHAPTER VIII.

RODBOROUGH

RODBOROUGH Church was a Chapel of Ease to Minchinhampton, the Rector of the latter Parish being obliged to provide a Curate to officiate in the Chapel, and there was also a Lectureship attached to the Church in the gift of Brasenose College, Oxford. In Rudder's time this Lectureship was worth £58 per ann., but of late years it has produced considerably more, owing to part of the endowment estate having become building land. The present Rector of Rodborough kindly informs me that in 1897 the interest in the Lectureship, and also the advowson of the Living, were bought and the purchase money raised on loan by the Lectureship Trustees. This loan will be paid off in eight years' time ; the Rector in the meantime receiving £50 a year from the Trustees.

In the reign of James I., the Parishioners of Rodborough petitioned for the Rector of Minchinhampton to find a Chaplain to officiate in the Chapel, and accordingly, by a decree in Chancery (2, James I., 1605), the Rector was bound to set aside £40 a year for a Curate and £5 for the repair of the Chapel. The only ancient part of the Church now remaining is the Tower, which is very good of its kind, and stands out beautifully on the side of the hill. The Church contains a Jacobean pulpit, the gift of Jasper Estcourt, in 1624, and also Communion Plate and Sanctuary chairs of the same date.

The Traffic in Pews.—Until it's restoration, Rodborough Church afforded a good illustration of the very common practice, in former times, of buying and selling Pews in Churches—a traffic which continued, in some cases, up to quite

recent times. Those who were authorised by the Churchwardens to erect Galleries and Pews for their occupation,
claimed them as their freehold within the Church, and in the
writer's recollection, both at Minchinhampton and Avening,
brass plates were fixed on many of the Pews recording that
" this Pew is the property of ——— "

There is a good example of this practice in the Parish
Books of Rodborough, where this entry occurs :—

" We, the Minister and substantial Freeholders and
Inhabitants of the Parish of Rodborough, did consent
and agree that Samuel Shurmer, one of our present churchwardens, should erect a gallery for his own use in the south-
east Ile of our Parish Church of Rodborough aforesaid,
which gallery is accordingly erected and is the property
of the said Samuel Shurmer. In witness whereof we
hereunto subscribed our hands in the year of our Lord,
1733.

PHIL SHEPPARD, Minister.
DAN. H. CHARGES, Churchwarden."

Then follow the signatures of 15 other parishioners.

There are many other records of the sale and purchase of
pews and seat places in Rodborough Church, and also a great
number in the Churchwardens' accounts of Minchinhampton,
beginning as early as 1632, when it was recorded "That Jeremie
Buck, senior, did at his owen proper cost and charges build
two seats for himself and his succeeding posteritye." William
Nichols and George Small again in 1664 built a gallery " at
their own propper cost and charge. And it is for their owen
use and those whom they lett it unto for ever." There were
also two proprietary galleries in Avening Church up to the time
of the recent restoration.

There is a quaint entry in the Rodborough records in
1748 relating to a dispute which had arisen as to the music
in the church, as follows :—

" That Peter Playne of Stroud Parish shall have
liberty to sit in the said Pew and make use of his Bassoon,
but that no other instrument but a Bassoon shall be
used there."

Profaning the Sabbath seems to have been severely
punished in the neighbourhood. Thus we read that Anthony

Keene, of Rodborough, was presented to the Court of the Hundred, in the reign of Elizabeth, for playing " Globos dies festivalibus "—presumably playing bowls on Sunday and feast days. There is also an entry of a fine for a similar offence in the Hampton Churchwardens' accounts for the year 1658 as follows :—

> " Received of Mr Samuel Sheppard, from the Sessions, as conviction money for profaning the Lord's Day, by Robert Woodroff and Edward Trevis, the summ of 6s 8d, and this money paid to Widdow Mills 2s, and to various other persons in smaller sums."

A very celebrated Gloucestershire man was born and lived in the Parish of Rodborough. Fosbroke says of him (Vol. I., p. 365) :—" Hill House is the superb residence of that distinguished Baronet, Sir George Onesiphorus Paul, in literature able and elegant, in forensic business very unlimited, etc."

Born in 1746, he became a gentleman Commoner of St. John's College, Oxford, and, after taking his degree, he travelled for two years in Europe, visiting almost every Country. Returning to England, he devoted himself to the business of his County, becoming High Sheriff in 1780, and Chairman of Quarter Sessions about the same time. But it is as a philanthropist and prison reformer that Sir George Paul is chiefly entitled to fame. [1]On his Cenotaph in Gloucester Cathedral it is recorded that he was " a man endeared to his friends by many virtues both public and private, but who claims this mark of local respect by having first reduced to practice the principles which have immortalised the name of Howard."

The late Mr Barwick Baker, of Hardwicke Court, himself a Reformer of world-wide reputation, says of him :—" In 1783, Sir George Paul, as Chairman of Quarter Sessions, brought the subject before our County and procured an Act of Parliament for building the Gloucester Gaol and Penitentiary. Sir George took the suggestions of Howard and carried them into practice. An address, published in 1792, gave notice of the completion of the Gaol and then commenced nearly the first attempt at improvement in the old barbarous system, and from the first became the model for nearly all the world." Sir George died Jan. 16, 1820, aged 74 years.

[1] " Good and Great Men of Gloucestershire," by Joseph Stratford, p. 457.

Hill House is now called Rodborough Manor, and is the property of Mr S. Marling. It was unfortunately burnt down a few years ago. Lord John Russell bought it in 1835, on being elected one of the Members of Parliament for Stroud, and on being created Earl Russell, he took his second title from the neighbouring village, Amberley.

Amberley and Brimscombe

In the year 1840, the ancient Parish of Minchinhampton was divided into three Ecclesiastical Districts, *viz.* :—The mother parish of Minchinhampton, Amberley, and Brimscombe. A Church was erected in each of the two latter districts by Mr David Ricardo, to whom the Advowsons of all three Livings belonged. There are no architectural features about either of the two new Churches, which were erected at an unfortunate time.

Rodborough also became a substantive Parish at this time, and the Advowson of the Living, as mentioned above, is now in the hands of Trustees.

MINCHINHAMPTON CHURCH (EXTERIOR)

CHAPTER IX.

MINCHINHAMPTON CHURCH

THERE is no evidence of a Church having stood at Hampton in Saxon times, though a Priest is mentioned in Domesday Book, and it is unlikely that there was more than a Chapel of some sort either at Hampton or at Avening before the Conquest.

Until recently, and within living memory, a considerable amount of Norman work remained at Hampton, and, of course, as we shall see later on, a very remarkable amount still exists at Avening. I have no record of the date of the Consecration of either Church, but Thomas, in his " Survey of Worcester," says that the great Altar in Minchinhampton Church was dedicated by Walter de Maydenstone, Bishop of Worcester, in July, 1315, though this must have been some time after the building of the main part of the Church.

Up to 1842, when Hampton Church underwent a ruthless " restoration," there remained on the north side of the Nave four arches upon circular pillars with indented capitals of undoubtedly Norman work ; and in the wall over these arches, during the rebuilding of the Nave, two small Norman windows were found, only six inches wide, deeply recessed and splayed, similar to those still to be seen in Avening Church. Of other Norman work there remained the wall below the East window and the North wall of the chancel in which were found, walled up, two windows similar to those already mentioned as being in the north wall of the Nave. The other parts of the ancient Church were of 14th century work, except a few alterations in the 16th century in a very debased style of architecture. The arches on the south side of the Nave were pointed and upon octagonal pillars. The Clerestory had late square-headed windows of two lights, and the brackets, which supported the beams of the roof, rested on large bold corbel heads. The Chancel of the old Church was considerably longer than the present one, and, together with the Nave, was destroyed in 1842.

Thus the only parts of ancient work remaining after this " restoration " were the tower and the north and south transepts, and even the beautiful window in the south transept would have shared the same fate but for the exertions of the late Dr. Dalton, of Dunkirk Manor, a fellow of the Society of Antiquaries, who successfully pleaded for its retention. Thus was saved this window, which is the chief glory of Minchinhampton Church, and the parish owes a deep debt of gratitude to the memory of Dr. Dalton for rescuing this treasure from the pickaxe of the " restorer." It was therefore allowed to remain, being only " improved " by taking away a very important transom. The south transept, which is 40 feet in length, 16 feet wide and 40 feet in height, is very remarkable, some of its features being almost unique. The roof is most singular, of high pitch, and arched in stone formed of a succession of strong ribs, each adorned with pierced work, and the intervals between each arched rib and the high pitched roof also fitted with pierced stone work. On the east and west side of this transept is a range of small two-light windows, set very closely together, with buttresses between them, corresponding exactly with the arched intervals of the ribs of the roof. The south window of this transept, already alluded to above, is very fine, and consists of a rose or wheel with eight radiating arms enclosing sixteen equilateral compartments. In the recesses of the south wall of this transept are two stone coffins under elaborately ornamented ogee conopies. The exposed sides of these coffins are relieved by quatrefoils, and on their lids are recumbent figures, one, that of a cross-legged knight, and the other that of a lady. The feet of the knight rest on a lion, and those of the lady on a dog, the emblem of fidelity.

The figures are of stone, and life size, and the hands of both are clasped in prayer. The knight is in a complete suit of armour, and wears a long surcoat, confined by a narrow girdle, and cut up in front, under which two tunics are to be seen, one slightly longer than the other and extending to the knee, also cut up in front. His shield, on which is the Crest of the de la Meres (an Eagle displayed) hangs at the left from a strap over the right shoulder. The sword hangs from a broad belt, buckling in front, and there are spur straps on the feet.

The lady wears a gown with long pointed sleeves, beneath which are others, tight to the wrist. The hair is padded at the sides, and she wears a wimple and kerchief, which has a fold coming from the back of the head to the front, where it is sewn down by a thread.[1]

Bigland says of these Monuments :—" In the reign of Richard II., 1382, Sir John de la Mere and Maud, his wife, rebuilt the south transept." But there was no Sir John de la Mere living at that time and holding land at Minchinhampton, and these Monuments no doubt represent either Sir Peter or his son, Sir Robert de la Mere (sometimes spelt de la Mare). From an Inquisition made at Chirinton (Cherington) on Saturday next before the Feast of St. Martin, 20 Edward 1 (1292), of the lands which were of Peter de la Mare, we find that, besides land at Cherington,

> " He also held certain lands and tenements at Hampton of the Abbot of Malmesbury and the Abbess of Cadamo (Caen) by soccage, paying, therefore, to the said Abbot 40s, and to the said Abbess 13s 4d. There is there a messuage, which, together with the garden, is worth, by the year, 6s 8d. There are 25 acres of arable land, price of the acre 2d, sum 4s 2d. There are there of the rent of the freemen by the year 6d. Sum total of Hampton 116s 10d, out of which there are paid as above, by the year, 53s, and so the sum is clear 63s 6d. The marriage of Robert, son and heir of the said Peter, is worth 100 marks."

There is also a very similar entry with regard to Robert, son of Peter, on Oct. 23, 1308, except that he held at Minchinhampton 40 acres of land, which is the amount now belonging to the Trustees of St. Loe's school, the ancient home of the de la Meres. The value is stated to be, after deductions, £8 8s 5d clear. Peter de la Mere, son of Robert, is stated to be " his next heir, and was aged 18 years on the feast of the Purification of the Blessed Mary last year." I believe that this Monument represents Sir Peter de la Mere, and that it

---

[1] B. & Gl. Archæol. Trans. Vol. XXVIII., p. 97.

was erected by his son, Sir Robert. The Tombs are evidently part of the original design, and, if my surmise is correct, the transept was built between 1292 and 1308, which was the year in which Sir Robert died, at the age of 34, and, therefore at a much earlier date than that given by Bigland.

In connection with this transept, a curious error has arisen, into which every County Historian from Atkyns downward has fallen. Atkyns, Rudder, and Bigland say that a Chantry was established by a person called Ansloe, or Ainslow, and that the monumental effigies are those of a knight of this name, and Fosbroke goes so far as to give as a reference the Patent roll of 12 Edward III., but on verifying this reference I find no mention of any name like Ansloe, but that a Chantry in honour of the Virgin Mary was established by the then Rector in 1338, 44 years before the date given by Bigland for the building of the transept by the de la Meres. This family held, for many generations, the estate on which St. Loe's School now stands, and I have no doubt that Mr Bruce's[1] view on this point is the correct one, *viz. :* that "Ansloe" is simply a corruption of St. Loe, and that "Ansloes Aisle " is, in reality, " St. Loe's Aisle," and, as we shall see later on, the Chantry established by William de Prestbury in 1338 was situated outside the Church.

The church tower presents rather a problem. Had it a spire, and if so, why was it finished off in its present state ? Both Atkyns and Rudder say it had a spire which was taken down half way, and ornamented with pinnacles. Bigland says, on the authority of two manuscript histories by Wantner and Parsons in the Bodleian Library, that the upper part of the spire was blown down in 1602, when it was finished with an embattled parapet. Fosbroke does not mention it. I have had these two MSS. copied, and find that Wantner, a most inaccurate historian, does indeed say : " It had formerly a spire upon the top thereof, which was thrown down by tempestious weather, and afterwards rebuilt as now it standeth." But he gives no date. Parsons, whose history is much more accurate than Wantner's, says :—" The spire steeple is in ye middle whose Top falling to decay was in part taken down." The churchwardens' accounts also seem to point to the spire having been lowered and not blown down.

[1] Extracts from the Churchwardens' accounts of Minchinhampton page 9.

MINCHINHAMPTON CHURCH SOUTH TRANSEPT
(INTERIOR)

In 1556 we read " to a man that say (saw) the Stepulle iijs iiijd." In 1560 " paid to Jhon Yngrow, Jhon Newman, & Henry pole for lettynge downe the stones out of the steeple ijs." There are many other payments to people who came to " loke upon the steeple." Finally, in 1563, one Thomas Slie, who appears to have been a master mason, of Painswick, and the " Plommer " received considerable sums of money for work on the steeple. There are also charges for " meat and drincke when the stones were carried."

On the whole I believe the spire had been in a dangerous condition for some time, and, after taking many opinions from those who came "to loke upon the Steeple," the churchwardens were ultimately compelled, very likely under pressure from the authorities at the Visitations, to undertake the work, in 1563, and I think we may be grateful to them for making so good a finish to the shortened spire.

On the restoration in 1842, when the old nave and chancel were broken down, a number of incised stone slabs were found in the 14th century walls, used as building material in various parts. By this means these stones had been preserved for some 500 years and handed down in a remarkably good state of preservation—the incisions of many of them being as sharply defined as when they were first cut from the softer beds of the great oolite weatherstone of the district. These incised gravestones appear to have been used not only as coverings for coffins, but also as memorial stones over the grave below, as only one early stone coffin was found, though there were some of a later date, notably one in a recess in the end of the wall of the north transept. This coffin, destroyed in 1842, contained a skeleton of an adult, together with traces of habiliments and " clouted shoes."

These ancient and beautifully-incised slabs were appropriated by the contractor at the 1842 restoration, and given to anyone who cared to have them. Thus they were scattered all over the neighbourhood and used for rockeries, ferneries, etc., or left lying in neglected corners of pleasure grounds. So that more has been done to efface these memorials of past years than had been accomplished in the previous five centuries.[1] Illustrations of some of these slabs are given on page 54.

[1] Mr G. F. Playne in Proceedings of the Cotteswold Naturalists' Field Club, v., 39-45

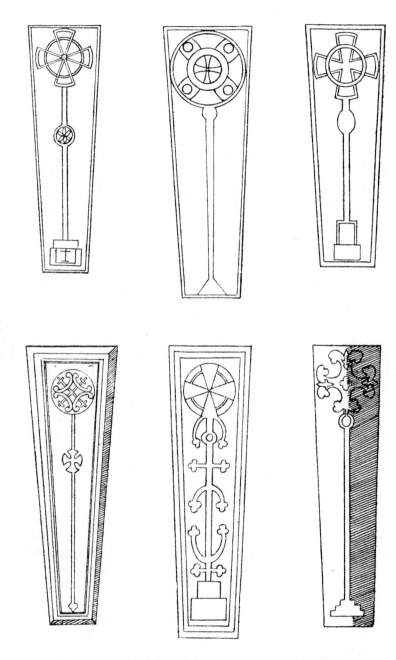

INCISED SLABS FOUND IN MINCHINHAMPTON CHURCH

MINCHINHAMPTON CHURCH SOUTH TRANSEPT
(EXTERIOR)

On removing the plaster and whitewash from the eastern end of the Nave, the ancient site of the Parish Altar was disclosed, in a precisely similar position to that at Avening. The pitch of the old Norman roof can also be seen, but it is a pity that black mortar was used in pointing the stones, which present a rather unsightly appearance. The Septum wall of Alabaster was added by the Rev. F. A. Mather, in place of the former one of stone, and the present pulpit, also of Alabaster, was erected by subscription, in memory of the Rev. E. C. Oldfield, replacing a fairly good one in stone. But I venture to think that it would have been more in keeping with the rest of the building to have carried out these alterations in the beautiful freestone of the district. The stripping of plaster also revealed the position of the ancient Roodloft, and the access to it is to be seen on the Tower stairs, through a doorway now walled up. The bells are six in number, all but one cast by the Rudhalls, the famous bellfounders, of Gloucester. The inscriptions are as follows :—

1. Peace and good neighbourhood Abraham Rudhall, 1719

2. Geo. Playne & Fras. Chambers
   (Churchwardens) ..   .. T. Mears, 1842

3. Prosperity to the Church of
   England (Nathaniel Perks
   and James Parker, Church-
   wardens) ..   ..   .. Abraham Rudhall, 1719

4. A. Townsend & G. Ralph,
   Churchwardens ..   .. John Rudhall, 1797

5. John Rowden, Curate   .. Abraham Rudhall, 1719

6. Jos Iles & Jacob Scuse,
   Churchwardens ..   .. John Rudhall, 1825

Coming to more recent times, we are glad to recognise that the iconoclasm of former days has passed away, let us hope for ever. The incongruities and disfigurements introduced in 1842 have been swept away, and the appearance of the interior of the Church has been greatly improved. When I first recollect it there were ugly galleries running along three sides of the Nave. The organ and choir were located in a huge gallery, which blocked up the whole west end of the Church. There was the inevitable " three decker," the Rector preaching in a black gown, below him the curate facing the congregation in the reading-desk, and below the Curate again the Clerk, who said the responses and gave out the hymns.

But when all this is admitted, it is not quite fair to blame too much the restorers of the Church, who did their best according to the lights and tastes of the day. Archæology was not studied in those days, and the architecture of the early Victorian age, of which very dreadful examples still remain with us, is truly deplorable. At any rate, nothing can be said against the structure of the building. The stone work is admirable, and reflects great credit on the local artificers, who executed it in the beautiful stone of the neighbourhood. I have no record of the amount expended on the restoration, but I have heard that it cost a large sum of money, which was generously subscribed by the parishioners, headed by Mr David Ricardo.

On the death of the Rev. Charles Whately, who had held the living since 1841, and the coming in 1865 of the Rev. E. C. Oldfield, a new era may be said to have begun in the history of the parish Church. One of the first improvements was the rebuilding of the east end of the Chancel, and the erection of a new large window in place of a very small and poor one placed there in 1842. The window was designed by the late Mr Burges, and is a double one with two panes of tracery about two feet apart. Mr Burges's reason for designing this double window was that the south transept window is so magnificent that he desired to introduce a special feature, giving more richness to the east window than could be done with a single one. The glass was executed by Messrs. Hardman, of Birmingham, from designs by Mr Powell. The lower part represents our Saviour's conflicts, and the upper part His triumph. The five principal lights represent : in the centre the Crucifixion ; on the left, washing the feet of the disciples, and the bearing of the Cross ; and on the right the Agony in the garden, and the Scourging. In the centre of the circle is Our Lord in glory seated on a throne ; the ten medallions represent prophets, apostles and martyrs. There is this inscription on a brass plate : " To the glory of God and to the Memory of Mary Ann, wife of William Playne, of Longfords, Esquire, this window was dedicated Anno Domini, 1869." Mrs Playne was killed in a carriage accident on May 20th, 1868. The whole of the cost of re-building the east end of the Church,

MINCHINHAMPTON CHURCH (INTERIOR, LOOKING EAST)

including the window and glass, was the gift of Mr William Playne.

The disfiguring side galleries were soon removed, not without considerable opposition from some of the older inhabitants, and a little later the cumbersome west gallery was pulled down, and the organ removed to its present position in the north transept. The choir-stalls were added and other improvements made, mostly at the expense of Mr Oldfield and members of his family.

In 1873, the beautiful south transept window had painted glass added to it ; this was also executed by Messrs. Hardman, and the design and general appearance of the window is most successful. It was dedicated by the late Mr H. D. Ricardo and his sister to the memory of their father and mother, and is intended to represent the work of the Holy Ghost. It bears the following inscription :—

" In honorem Sanctissimae Trinitatis, et in piam parentum memoriam hanc fenestram ornandam curavere Henricus David Ricardo et soror ejus.—A.D. MDCCCLXXIII."

The west window and the south windows of the Nave have also recently had painted glass added to them, designed and executed by Mr Herbert Bryans, the brother of the late Rector. The west window was the gift of the Rev. E. L. Bryans. The others are memorials of Mr Edward Playne, Mr and Mrs C. R. Baynes, Mr and Mrs H. D. Ricardo, and Mr and Mrs George Playne. There is also a window in the south transept in memory of George Edward, son of Mr and Mrs Edward Playne.

The Church as it stands now is a noble monument of the piety of our forefathers, and though we may regret the disappearance of some features which we should have wished to retain, we may nevertheless be thankful that so much of the ancient fabric still remains.

CHAPTER X.

EPIDEMIC OF FEVER IN MINCHINHAMPTON

A S has already been stated, the restoration of Minchinhampton Church was begun in 1842 and finished in the latter part of the following year. The lowering of the level of the Nave and of a considerable part of the Churchyard, necessitated the removal of a very large number of bodies, buried under the pavement of the Church, and in the crowded Churchyard outside. These burials of a large population both within and without the Church had been continuous for 500 years, and, until the enlargement of the Churchyard a few years ago, gruesome and horrible sights were to be seen when a grave was dug in the old and more crowded part. Those who remember the state of things at the restoration of Avening Church, where everything possible was done to avoid any risk to the health of the inhabitants, can imagine the condition of matters at Minchinhampton, where far more movement of soil was necessary, and no care whatever was taken. The soil thrown up by the excavations appears to have been left in heaps in the adjoining fields for any one who cared to use it to carry away. Some was spread on pasture land or taken away and used as garden manure. This was the case at the Rectory, with disastrous consequences, as we shall see later on.

Dr. Daniel Smith, a medical practitioner at Minchinhampton, writing to Dr. Southwood Smith, who was Medical Officer to the recently established " Health of Towns Association," gives the following account of the epidemic :—

" Our town is situated on a considerable elevation ; each shower of rain produces its little torrent, which passes through the streets with a considerable power ; our streets are wide, and the inhabitants tolerably (!) cleanly ; no offensive business being carried on, and the place is proverbial for health. I have practised as a surgeon here for sixteen years, and, until the last two years I have no recollection of having had a single case of typhus fever. In the latter end of the year 1844 I had many cases uniform in their symptoms and a disposition to assume the typhoid type. Last year very few occurred. Within the last two months we have had upwards of 150, so as to induce a general meeting of the inhabitants. The fever is identical with that of the former year, but more severe ; cold rigors, congestion of the brain, great prostration of the vital powers, blood dark, with delirium on the second or third day, are the early symptoms." Dr. Smith goes on to state that hundreds of loads of very dark earth mixed with bones removed from the Churchyard still remained within 50 yards of the town. Many cartloads of similar soil were taken to the Rectory, and used as manure for the garden and shrubberies, with the consequence that out of the Rector's family, consisting of himself, his wife and two children, the wife and one child took the fever and died, and the gardener, who used the manure, shortly after also died of the same disease.

Throughout the whole epidemic, the outlying hamlets were quite free from fever, and only the town of Minchinhampton was affected. A wordy warfare then ensued, beginning with the letter of Dr. Daniel Smith, quoted above, in November, 1846, and continuing until the end of February, 1847. The letters appeared mostly in the *Gloucester Journal*, and the controversy was also taken up by the London papers, the *Times*, the *Sun*, and the *Daily News*, until the fever at Minchinhampton became notorious all over the country.

The Parish took sides. One party included Mr David Ricardo, the Patron of the living, Mr Bruce, of Hyde House, the transcriber of the Churchwardens' Accounts, and others, many of whom used the Churchyard soil as manure for their gardens and fields. On the other side were Dr Daniel Smith, Dr. Southwood Smith, Mr J. G. Ball, who lived at Minchinhampton, and was a solicitor and Coroner (as his son, Mr Morton Ball, now is), and also most of those who suffered in person or family from the epidemic. The correspondence became very acrimonious until the editors of the newspapers refused to publish any further letters on the subject of the epidemic.

An evidence of the carelessness with which exhumations were carried out, came under my notice when I was Churchwarden in the year 1872. In a cellar adjoining the Sexton's house, the bones of a large number of persons were found, evidently remains brought from the Church or Churchyard at the time of the restoration, thirty years before. My co-churchwarden and I, caused a deep trench to be dug in the Churchyard, and these remains were carefully collected and re-interred in the trench. This was done at night, and we agreed to say nothing about it, but as more than a generation has passed away since that time there is no harm in mentioning it now as an instance of the carelessness with which the removal of the bodies was carried out. The exhumations and dispersal of the remains caused very bitter feelings amongst the inhabitants, as the following extract from a long, contemporary, poetical effusion will show :—

"As late I sought my parents earthly goal
        To bow again where often I have knelt,
And breathe my vows and feel the love I felt,
        But lo ! appears to my astonished eyes
Things wondrous strange ; there I beheld arise
        Where stood the old and venerated Church
A fabric new to baulk my pious search,
        " Confusion worse confounded " spread around—
Sculls, epitaphs and coffins strewed around ;
        And ye dear valued ones—bone of my bone,
Flesh of my flesh—alas ye too were gone,
        Your sacred consecrated dust unshrined
And cast as worthless to the blasting wind.
        Nor stood I lonely in my speechless woe,
A widow's frenzied tears were seen to flow
        Upon the vacant spot where late found rest
The idol lover of her virgin breast.
        And weeping brothers, sisters, parents blend
Sighs, groans and tears bemoaning some dear friend
        Swept by sacrilegious deed away
To find a meaner grave in common clay."

Typhoid or enteric fever was only imperfectly understood in those days, and all diseases of this type went by the generic name of " Typhus," which is in fact a different form of fever, and now much less common than typhoid. Typhus was the well-known " Jail fever," the infection of which was frequently brought by prisoners from the old insanitary gaols and communicated to Judges, Jurymen, Barristers, often with fatal effects, whence the Assizes where this occurred went by the name of " Black Assizes." The custom also, which continued till recent times, of placing rue and other herbs on the rail of the dock was due to this fear.

There is no doubt from contemporary accounts that the Minchinhampton epidemic was typhoid fever, and it is strange that the most probable immediate cause of the outbreak is not even mentioned in any of the correspondence.

It is now known that typhoid fever is mainly caused by the pollution of drinking water by the " bacillus typhosus." It may be produced by dust, but, as the bacillus lives only for a few hours when exposed to sun and air, this is not a very common means by which it is produced. The bacillus will live for many weeks covered up by ordinary soil moistened by rain, and it multiplies exceedingly.[1] The great oolite formation greatly favours the pollution of water if there is any contamination of the soil above. The rock is rent by vertical fissures, locally called " lizens," through which the rainfall finds its way to the fuller's earth, where the springs burst out. These " lizens " have from time immemorial been largely used for drainage purposes, for which they were very convenient, thereby doing away with all necessity for an expensive system of drainage. Any liquid, however contaminated, was turned into a " lizen," and when out of sight was soon out of mind. Fortunately this system of drainage is now made illegal by the byelaws recently adopted by the Rural District Council. But at the time of the Minchinhampton epidemic it was an almost universal practice, and it is wonderful that there is no record of any previous epidemic having occurred in the town except a small one in the year 1758. The inhabitants were partly dependent for their water on wells which in the crowded parts of the town were greatly polluted and partly on the spring in the Wellhill, which, on analysis, was declared to be quite unfit for drinking purposes. The town is now amply supplied with excellent water by the Stroud Water Company, and most of the old wells have been closed.

CREMATION OR "ASHES TO ASHES."

The history of this epidemic and the facts detailed above, bring me to the subject of cremation, and I must at once make

---

[1] See Chapter 2.

it clear that what I say on this subject only represents my own views on a very controversial topic, and I am well aware that many will not agree with the conclusions at which I have arrived after considerable study of the subject.

It is not necessary to go deeply into the early history of cremation. It was practised by the Greeks, the Romans, and many other nations of antiquity. The Egyptians were an exception, as they embalmed and mummified their dead, but in their case they had a climate which favoured this system, and the scarcity of fuel would have rendered cremation on a large scale impossible in ancient Egypt. In England and on the Continent the practice has been growing year by year, and old prejudices are gradually giving way to more enlightened views. In 1874, the Cremation Society was inaugurated, the first President being Sir Henry Thompson, and all the Members of the Society subscribe on election to the following declaration : " We disapprove the present custom of burying the dead and desire to substitute some mode, which shall rapidly resolve the body into its component elements by a process which cannot offend the living, and shall render the remains absolutely innocuous. Until some better method is devised we desire to adopt that usually known as cremation." There is no doubt that the practice of cremation in modern Europe was at first stopped, and has since been in a great measure prevented by the Christian doctrine of the resurrection of the body. But this objection to cremation was disposed of by the philanthropist, Lord Shaftesbury, when he asked : " What would in such a case become of the blessed martyrs ? " Many clergymen, however, have been prominent in favour of cremation, notably the late Mr Haweis in his "Ashes to Ashes."[1]

Cremation after all is only hastening the process of nature and it surely is far less repulsive to think of the bodies of those we have loved on earth as " quickly resolved into their component parts " by cremation than left to the slow process of putrefaction. Meanwhile, cemeteries are becoming overcrowded, and every year it becomes increasingly difficult to find land suitable for their extension, and I look forward with confidence to the time when every county and every large town will have its Crematorium.

[1] Encylopædia Brittanica. Article, Cremation.

CHAPTER XI.

MONUMENTS IN MINCHINHAMPTON CHURCH AND CHURCHYARD

With reference to John Hampton's Brass, in Minchinhampton Church, Mr Cecil T. Davis, in his " Monumental Brasses of Gloucestershire,"[1] says :—

" On the Continent it was customary to represent the deceased enshrouded, even as early as the 14th Century. An example may be seen at Bruges (alas ! what is left of it now ?) of the date 1339, and very probably this fashion was introduced from the Continent, where it found much favour. Below the inscription are two groups of children, six sons under the father and three daughters under the mother. The eldest son is clothed in the garb of a Monk. This is very interesting, as brasses of Monks are seldom met with. This is not to be wondered at considering the vow made by them on entering the Order, and especially the one of poverty, by which they were bound. This son, whose name is not given, wears the Tonsure and closely cropped hair, a large hood or Cowl, and a long vestment with long open sleeves similar to the surplice sleeves of that date. The four remaining sons wear a loose fitting gown, without fur sleeves, and have long hair.

The eldest daughter Alice is dressed as a Nun. She wears the veil head-dress, a cape over her shoulders, open in front, revealing her gown with tight sleeves and girt by a loose girdle from which hangs a Rosary of 14 beads."

[1] p. 110.

Another very interesting Brass is that of Edward Halyday and his wife Margery, with a Merchant's Mark below, dated 1519. As these costumes are interesting, I quote Mr Davis's description of them.

" Edward Halyday has long clubbed hair covering the ears with a fringe, and he is clean shaven. His outer garment consists of a loose gown reaching to his ankles ; it is thrown open both above and below the waist, exposing to view the fur lining. The sleeves of the gown are loose and hanging round the cuffs is a broad band of fur. Beneath the gown the under dress is seen fitting closely to the neck, and the tight fitting sleeves of the same are to be seen at the wrists. He wears broad toed shoes, which are fastened across the instep.

Margery Halyday is represented in the then fashionable "kennel" or pedimental headdress ; the left hand front lappet is the only one shown and this is embroidered. She wears a tight fitting dress with a narrow collar. The lower portion is so arranged as to show the toes of her round shoes.

The sleeves have large reflex cuffs lined with fur. The broad loose hip girdle instead of being buckled terminates in three rosettes, and from these hang a metal chain, to which is fastened a metal pendant. There were formerly scrolls issuing from the mouths of both figures, bearing Latin inscriptions. On the man's :— " 𝔐𝔦𝔰𝔢𝔯𝔢 𝔪𝔢𝔦 𝔡𝔢 𝔰𝔠𝔡𝔪 𝔪𝔞𝔤𝔫𝔞 𝔪'𝔠𝔬𝔯𝔡𝔦𝔞 𝔱𝔲𝔞." On the wife's :— " 𝔍𝔩𝔩𝔲𝔦𝔢𝔱 𝔳𝔲𝔩𝔱𝔲 𝔰𝔲𝔲 𝔰𝔲𝔭' 𝔫𝔬𝔰 & 𝔪𝔦𝔰'𝔢𝔞𝔱𝔯 𝔫'𝔯𝔦." i.e., "Let his countenance lighten upon us and pity us." Beneath is the following inscription on the brass plate :—

" 𝔒𝔣𝔣 𝔭𝔬𝔯 𝔠𝔥𝔞𝔯𝔦𝔱𝔢 𝔭𝔯𝔞𝔭 𝔣𝔬𝔯 𝔱𝔥𝔢 𝔰𝔬𝔲𝔩𝔢 𝔬𝔣 𝔈𝔡𝔴𝔞𝔯𝔡𝔢 𝔥𝔞𝔩𝔭𝔡𝔞𝔭𝔢 𝔞𝔫𝔡 𝔐𝔞𝔯𝔤𝔢𝔯𝔭 𝔥𝔦𝔰 𝔚𝔭𝔣 𝔴𝔥𝔦𝔠𝔥 𝔈𝔡𝔴𝔞𝔯𝔡 𝔡𝔢𝔠𝔢𝔰𝔰𝔦𝔡 𝔱𝔥𝔢 𝔳𝔦𝔊𝔠. 𝔳𝔦 𝔡𝔞𝔭 𝔬𝔣 𝔄𝔭𝔯𝔦𝔩𝔩 𝔄𝔬 𝔡𝔫𝔦 𝔐𝔬𝔠𝔠𝔠𝔠𝔠𝔯𝔦𝔯."

Below is a Merchant's Mark engraved on a disk, and represents a double cross on a globe with the letters " E.H." When this brass was relaid the Merchant's Mark was placed upside down."

The figures are disproportionate in size, the effigy of the wife hardly reaching to her husband's shoulder. They are both erect, with hands together in supplication. Edward

BRASS OF EDWARD HALYDAY AND MARGERY HIS WIFE

Halyday is full face, whilst Margery is turned to her right, so as to look towards her husband.

The Wills of both Edward and Margery Halyday are in the Archives of the Prerogative Court of Canterbury. Some of the bequests are very quaint.

Edward is described as being of Rodborough, in the parish of Minchinhampton, Clothworker, and the Will is dated April 4th, 1519, two days before his death, as recorded on the Brass.

After directing that he is to be buried in the Parish Church of Minchinhampton, " nigh unto the sepulchre of my father and mother," he gives to the Parish Church xis. To every place of " Freres " within the Town of Gloucester and in the suburbs of the same, xiijs. iijd. To the prisoners in or about the town of Gloucester, vs. viiid. To the Chapel of Rodborough aforesaid, towards the buying of a pair of Vestments for the said Chapel, xis. To the Church of Stonehouse, towards the covering of the said Church of lead, xis. To his sons Edward, Richard, William and Michael, xil. each. To his daughters Agnes, Catherine, Elizabeth and Alianore, xil, " when each of them shall come to the years of maturity to be married ; that is, at the age of 18." He mentions land at Pakenhill and a farm at Stonehouse, which his wife is to occupy and enjoy " upon the condition that she be bound in law to his brother, William Halyday, to find a commendable priest to say Mass and other Divine services in the Parish Church of Minchinhampton, giving yearly unto the said Priest £5 6s 8d to pray for me and Margery, my wife, our fathers' and mothers' souls, and of all them that we be bound by the order of Charity to pray for." He makes his wife sole executrix, and his brother William overseer of his testament.

Margery bequeaths to the Mother Church of Worcester, xijd. To Minchinhampton in recompense of tythings forgotten, xxs. To an honest Priest to pray specially for her husband's soul and her own, and the soul of her benefactors, £5 vjs viijd. To Eleanor, her daughter, her best " bedis " and her best gown. " To Johan Halyday, wife of Henry Halyday, a certain portion of my raiment. To Johan Haydon my brass pot and pannys and pewter, except my London pewter. To the said Johan Haydon ij flock beds, with blankets and sheets to the said beds. She leaves £10 in the hands of her sons, Edward and William, for the continuance of an Anniversary for her husband and herself and their benefactors by the space of xiiij years. She gives to Tetbury Church to the common use of it iijs iiijd. She also mentions certain debts which she forgives, and leaves some small legacies to her godchildren. She leaves her sons Edward and William executors.

The Halydays survived for several generations at Hampton, and a Michael Halyday presented to the Living in 1618, having probably bought the next presentation from Lord Windsor. I do not know at what Mill Edward Halyday carried on his clothing business, but I am inclined to think that it was at Frome Hall, where a Halyday, also a clothier, lived, keeping, by the way, a pack of harriers, with which the writer's father frequently hunted as a boy in the early part of the 19th Century.

There is another Brass which may be of rather earlier date than the foregoing. It represents a civilian and wife, and it is believed there were originally two wives, one on each side of the man, but one of the wives has disappeared, and also the name and date. The costume is much the same as that of Edward Halyday and his wife, except that the toes of the man's boots are very wide and misshapen. In the XV. century, laws were made against the excessive length of shoes and in the XVI. century, the fashion had gone to the other extreme, and boots and shoes were so excessively square toed that the law, which had formerly limited the length, was now called in to abridge the width of these pedal terminations. (Planché's Cyclopædia of Costume). Below is rather a mutilated inscription, which seems to be :—

" **De' miserat' n'ri &......dicat nobis.**"

By far the most distinguished man who lies buried at Minchinhampton is Dr. James Bradley, in memory of whom there is this inscription, translated from the original Latin, engraved on a brass-plate in the south transept, formerly in the Churchyard :—

" Here lies buried James Bradley, D.D., a member of the Royal Societies of London, Paris,[1] Berlin, and

---

[1] The original Latin is " Lutetiæ Parisorum." Lutetia was the name in Roman times of an Island in the Seine, inhabited by the Parisi, a small Gallic tribe, and now incorporated in the City of Paris. Lutetia continued to be the Latin name for Paris until comparatively recent times.

Tho. Hudson pinx.   J. Faber Fecit.

Jacobus Bradley, S.T.P.

Regalis Societatis Socius.

Astronomus Regius *et apud* Oxonienses

Astronomiæ Professor Savilianus.

Emery Walker Ph. sc.

JACOBUS BRADLEY, S.T.P.

St. Petersburg, Astronomer Royal, Savilian Professor of Astronomy at Oxford. A man highly esteemed for his knowledge of Physical Science and principally in the elucidation of the most abstruse points ; so successfully diligent, and of such great wisdom, that all those who devoted themselves to these pursuits freely owned his superiority ; and at the same time of such modesty that he alone seemed ignorant of the high reputation in which he was held by those most competent to judge. He died July 12th, 1762, aged 70."

Dr. Bradley was born at Sherborne, Gloucestershire, in March, 1693, and took orders in 1719, but resigned his ecclesiastical preferments on being appointed Savilian Professor of Astronomy at Oxford. He had been elected a fellow of the Royal Society in 1718, and was appointed Astronomer Royal in 1742, succeeding the celebrated Edmund Halley. After a most distinguished career he retired on a crown pension of £250 a year, and died in broken health at Chalford, within the parish of Minchinhampton. Bradley's great discovery of the " aberration of light," a corner stone of astronomical science, and of the nutation of the earth's axis, will make his name famous for all time. It is a pity that a poor brass plate is the only memorial of so great a Gloucestershire man, but both the Government and the Royal Society have been appealed to in vain for a contribution towards a more adequate one.

Dr. Bradley's mother and sister are also buried at Minchinhampton.

There is an alliterative inscription to the memory of Jeremiah Buck, the elder, each line beginning with a letter of his name :—

I.   Intombed here lies a Pillar of the State
E.   Each good man's friend to the Poor
      Compassionate

and so on, but the Poetry is not of such a quality as to make it worth while to quote further.

There is also a rather pathetic inscription in Latin to the memory of Philip, only son of George Ridpath. He is described as " a youth of the greatest promise, learned beyond his years, of a keen intelligence, an excellent disposition, and highly endowed with many other gifts. With the consent of his parents, and by the advice of the Doctors, he left London for the country, and, on the journey to Gloucester, he was taken suddenly ill on July 3rd, 1705, and early the following morning in this town " animam piam et puram Deo reddidit," in the 22nd year of his age.

There are many monuments both in the Church and in the Churchyard to members of the Sheppard family, all ascribing untold virtues to the departed. The specimen already given of the Epitaph on Samuel Sheppard will serve as an example of the others.

There are also many memorials of the Pinfolds, who were a noted family of clothiers for many generations. Edward Pinfold, in 1683, built the picturesque gabled house known as " The Iron Mills," in the possession of the writer ; the date stone, with the initials E.P.M. for Edward and Mary Pinfold, is over the entrance, and the date is also recorded on an illuminated Sundial fixed on the south wall of the house.

Space will not admit of more epitaphs being given, though many are of great interest, but of inordinate length, according to the fashion of the 17th and 18th centuries. There are many memorials of the Iles's, Cambridges, and Clutterbucks, etc., and also several to the memory of the Bucks, of whom we shall have a great deal to say later on. Many of the tombs and inscriptions were destroyed in 1842, but fortunately the diligence of Bigland has preserved all that were legible in his day.

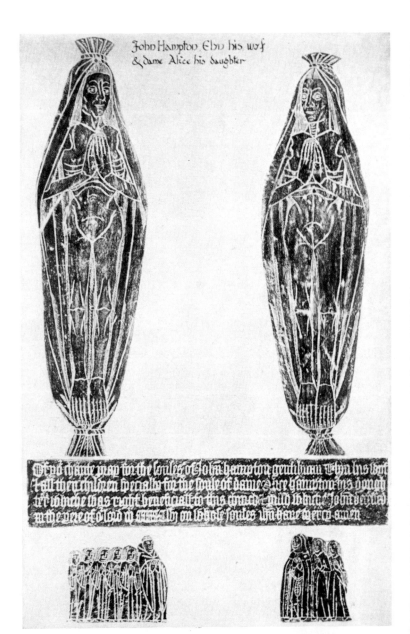

BRASS OF JOHN HAMPTON, HIS WIFE AND CHILDREN

CHAPTER XII.

LADY ALICIA HAMPTON OR DAME ALICE HAMPTON

IT has always been supposed that Dame Alice Hampton was a Nun of Syon, probably because on her Memorial Brass she is depicted in the Monastic dress. The present Lady Abbess of Syon, however, informs me that this is not so, but that Dame Alice was a " Sister of the Chapter," and not a professed Nun. In the necrology of the Abbey, an entry occurs : " Sep. 27, 1516, Lady Alicia Hampton, Benefactress," and the Lady Abbess says : " The Anniversaries of all entered in the Necrology are read out in the Chapter House the morning before they occur in order that the suffrages may be offered for them. For four centuries Lady Alice Hampton's Anniversary has thus been announced at Syon, on the morning of every 26th of September as occurring on the morrow, the 27th." This remarkable tribute to a Benefactress also clears up an obscure point as to the date of the inscription on the Hampton Brass in Minchinhampton Church, which is in old English character, as in the illustration :—

" Of pooᵣ charite pray for the soules of John Hampton, gentilman, Glyn, his wyf & all their children, specially for the soule of Dame Alice Hampton, his daughter, whiche was right beneficiall to this Church & p'ish, which John. deceßed, in the pere of oᵣ Lord, Mo. C.C.C.C.C.L.B.J., on whose soules ihu haue mercy. Amen."

With reference to the date of the above, Mr Haines, in his " Manual of Monumental Brasses," says :—" Though the date on this Brass is 1556, it was engraved about 1510, and the date subsequently added." Mr Cecil T. Davis, in "Monumental Brasses," p. 113, says :—"The letters C.L.V.J. were evidently added at a later period, so that the Brass may have been engraved at an earlier date even than that assigned by Mr Haines, possibly at the end of the 15th century." It was no uncommon thing for the main part of a Brass to be engraved before the death of the person commemorated and the date subsequently added carelessly by some one else in later times. It is a little uncertain who John Hampton was, the name not being an uncommon one in the county. A Sir William Hampton, born at Minchinhampton, became a Member of the Fishmongers Company, and Lord Mayor of London in 1472, and is said to have been the first to set up Stocks in every Ward for the punishment of vagabonds, male and female. I am inclined to think that John Hampton was the son of Sir William, and consequently Dame Alice was his grand-daughter. Probably the eldest son, being in orders, could not inherit, and the rest of the family may have died young, which was a very common occurrence in those days ; at any rate, we do not find the name again at Minchinhampton after the death of Alice, and she undoubtedly inherited considerable wealth on the death of her father.

There is a very interesting Memorial of Dame Alice Hampton at Longfords, where a turret clock, made in 1806 by Jones, of Chalford,[1] has ever since that date struck, and still strikes, the hour and quarters on a bell with the following inscription : "Dame Alys Hamton, AoMLVeXv," as in the illustration. The preposition "de" in this inscription has been partially erased by lines filed across it, in all probability by Dame Alice's direction, her name not having the prefix "de." I do not know the whole history of this very early bell, which was, apparently, cast in 1515, the year before Dame Alice's death, which, as already stated, occurred on Sep. 27th, 1516. The bell was formerly fixed on the so-called "Second Market House," there being no less than three in Minchinhampton, as we shall see later on, and when the "second" was pulled down in 1806 and the materials sold, the bell was bought by the writer's grandfather and placed in its present position. The Lady Abbess of Syon, writing of it, says : "I am glad that through your grandfather, the bell was

---

[1] Jones of Chalford was a very celebrated Clockmaker in his day, and I have a very fine Chime Clock made by him in 1804, playing one of four tunes every four hours.

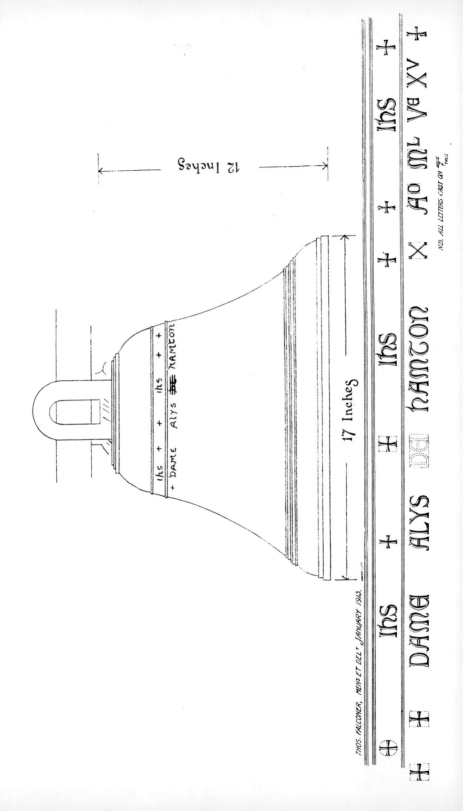

THOS. FALCONER, MENS ET DEL.T JANUARY 1943.

12 Inches

17 Inches

+ DAME ALYS ᛘᛖ ᚾAMTON

ihs + ihs +

N.B. ALL LETTERS CAST ON THUS

DAMA ALYS DEL ᚾAMTON OF M LV XV

ihs ihs ihs

saved, otherwise it might have been lost to Hampton. Lady Alicia Hampton little thought that, four hundred years from the date of the gift, it would be a means of communication between Hampton and Syon, which had ceased for more than three centuries and a half." I do not know for certain where the bell was placed before being transferred to the second Market House, or what purpose it served when there. It may have been used as a school bell, if a school was established there, as was the case in the present Market House, until very recent times. Originally it was probably a Sanctus bell, and may have been placed on a Chantry founded and endowed by William Prestbury, Rector of Minchinhampton, in 1338, " in a Chapell situate within the p'ish (parish) churche yarde." All traces of this chapel have disappeared.

Whilst dealing with the story of Dame Alice Hampton, mention must be made of the well-known tradition that she gave Minchinhampton Common to the inhabitants of the Parish. With every wish to find this tradition true, I regret to say that, not only is there no evidence to prove it, but there is much to show that Dame Alice never could have owned Minchinhampton Common, and therefore could not have given it to the Parishioners. As already mentioned, Dame Alice probably held a lease of the Manor for her life, but this would give her no power to alienate it. The Manor undoubtedly belonged to the Abbey of Syon up to the time of the Dissolution of the Monasteries long after the death of Dame Alice. Some benefactions given by her to Minchinhampton are mentioned in the " Valor Ecclesiasticus," 26, Henry VIII., 1534, as follows :—

"Money paid in alms to three poor persons in a certain almshouse to wit : To each of them 7d per week from the foundation of Lady Alicia Hampton, together for delivery and carriage of eight loads of wood annually for the same poor persons as appears by the declaration thereof mentioned £4 14s 9d."

There were probably other benefactions by Dame Alice, both to the Church and to the Parish. But if so they disappeared during the upheaval caused by the Reformation, and by the zeal of the Reformers to copy the example of the King in confiscating for their own benefit the endowments of the old religion.

There is not much more to be said about the manors of Avening and Minchinhampton until their final separation. The decline of the power and authority of the Lord of the Manor, which had already begun in the 15th century, continued, and many of their privileges were gradually abolished or fell into disuse. Courts Leet were and are still held, especially in manors where there is much waste land or commons, but, as many of these were from time to time enclosed, the utility of the Courts disappeared, and consequently they ceased to be held. Encroachments were still dealt with where the courts continued, and in Minchinhampton especially the rights of the commoners have been jealously guarded from generation to generation. Although there were in former times many encroachments, the rights of the commoners have, on the whole, been well maintained, and it is now, at the time at which I write, placed beyond the power of anyone to encroach upon the waste or common lands of the manor, by the transference of the rights of the Lord of the Manor to the National Society for the preservation of Open Spaces, etc.

The two Manors remained in the possession of the descendants of Samuel Sheppard for many generations, until the year 1812, when the writer's grandfather, William Playne, bought the Manor of Avening, with a considerable amount of property in that parish, which still remains in the possession of his descendants, and, in 1814, Mr David Ricardo, the eminent writer on Political Economy, whose works are still standard classics, bought the Manor of Minchinhampton, with a large estate, and the beautiful residence of Gatcombe Park, now the seat of his great grandson, Major Ricardo. Thus the two Manors of Minchinhampton and Avening were finally separated, and the connection which had survived for over seven centuries was dissolved.

CHAPTER XIII.

THE RECTORS OF MINCHINHAMPTON

IT is possible to give a fairly complete list of the Rectors of Minchinhampton from Papal Registers, the Worcester Episcopal Registers, and the Patent Rolls, but the names of the Chantry Priests are to a great extent lost, and only an occasional one appears here and there. I propose first to deal with the Rectors, and afterwards to record what can be gleaned as to the Chantries, and the Chantry Priests. The following is a list of the Rectors in chronological order, giving the dates of their institution so far as can be ascertained, and also any facts connected with their lives and ministry which can be gathered :—

1. MASTER ROGER DE SALANGES, A.D., 1260. He was appointed by the Abbess of Caen, and appears to have been a pluralist, as is shewn by the following entry in the papal registers :—

"Dispensation to Master Roger de Salange, Rector of Boketon, in the Diocese of Norwich, to hold also the Rectory of Menecheriehampton, in the Diocese of Worcester."

2. JORDAN DE WOLVERYNHAMPTON (Wolverhampton), A.D., 1282, presented by the Abbess of Caen. This Rector was also Sub-dean of Worcester, so presented by Godfrey Gifford, Bishop of Worcester, 1268-1301.

3. WILLIAM DE PRESTBURY, A.D., 1318, presented by the Abbess of Caen. He held the living until 1349, and was a

benefactor to the Church.   In the Patent Rolls 12 Edwd. III.
(1338), this entry occurs :—

> "16 Feb., 1338, license to alienate in Mortmain to
> William de Prestbury, parson of the Church of Munchene-
> hampton, co. Gloucester, two messuages, a toft, a water
> mill, 2½ virgates of land, and 20s rent in Munchenehampton
> for a Chaplain to celebrate divine service daily in honour
> of the Virgin Mary."

This foundation is all the more creditable to the
Rector, who, if we may judge from the following extract,
was not possessed of much ready money :—

> "John de Rous, Knight, William de Prestbury,
> parson of Munchenehampton, and John de Elkeston,
> acknowledge that they owe to Aylmer de Valentia, Earl
> of Pembroke, £80, to be levied in default of payment on
> their lands and chattels in counties Gloucester and
> Hereford."

This Chantry, as we shall see later on, continued to be
served up to the time of the Reformation.

Three Rectors now follow in quick succession, all appointed by the King in the year 1349, owing to the temporalities
of the Abbey of Caen being in his hands during the war in
France.   Why two of them held the living for so short a time
is not known, but possibly they moved to " better themselves."

4. STEPHEN MAULEON, May 8, 1349.

5. JOHN DE HOUTON, June 9, 1349.

6. JOHN DE MIDDLETON, August 18, 1349.   He held the
living till 1360, and is said to have also held the Canonry of
Wingham, with the expectation of a prebend.

7. THOMAS DE TOUCESTRE, Sept. 6, 1360.   He had been
parson of Rushenden, in the Isle of Sheppey.

8. WILLIAM DE FERRIBY, Oct. 3, 1360.   Appointed by
the King (Edward III.)

9. WILLIAM POTYN, of whom I know nothing, except the
exchange below.

10. MATTHEW HARSFELD, Dec. 4, 1377.   Was parson of
the Church of Slymbrigg (Slimbridge), and exchanged livings
with William Potyn.

11. ALAN LEVERTON, Sept. 30, 1390, " King's Clerk."

12. RICHARD ALKERINGTON, March 11, 1393 ; Doctor of Theology, exchanged livings with Thomas Wysebeck.

13. THOMAS WYSEBECK, Feb. 22, 1407. Parson of the Church of Herford, otherwise Hertfeld, in the Diocese of Chichester, exchanged as above. There appears to have been a general unrest amongst the clergy at this time, as, besides those above-mentioned, we have another exchange in the same year.

14. WILLIAM MAGOT, June 14, 1407. Parson of the Church of Beryk St. John, in the diocese of Salisbury, on an exchange of benefices with Thomas Wysebeck.

15. JOHN WODEFORD, March 18, 1411. Vicar of the Church of Asshton, in the Diocese of Salisbury, on exchange of benefices with William Magot.

16. ROBERT LOVER, Feb. 12, 1417.

17. RICHARD WILLYS, August 13, 1441. Instituted at the " King's College of Eton, near Windsor," by John Carpenter, Bishop of Worcester ; presented by the Earl of Suffolk, to whom the presentation had been given on the confiscation of the temporalities of the alien Convent of Caen.

18. WILLIAM GYAN, LL.B., 1456. Canon residentiary of the Cathedral Church of Sarum ; appointed by the Abbess and Convent of Syon. Resigned 1489. This is the first mention of the appointment of a Rector of Minchinhampton by the Abbess of Syon.

19. RICHARD GYAN, Feb. 27, 1489. Appointed by the Abbess and Convent of Syon, on the resignation of the fore-going.

20. JOHN READE, Bachelor in Theology, 1507. Appointed by the Abbess and Convent of Syon.

21. THOMAS POWELL, 1538. Appointed by the Abbess (Agnes Jordan) and Convent of Syon. "Agnes Dei patientiâ Abbatissa Syon presentavit, 1538."

22. GILBERT BOURNE, 1551. Appointed by Sir Edmund Peckham,[1] by assignment of a grant from Agnes, Abbess of Syon, 1539.

[1] Sir Edmund Peckham was Lord of the Manor of Denham, Bucks., to which place, as before mentioned, Agnes Jordan retired, after the confiscation of Syon Abbey, by Henry VIII.

Dr. Gilbert Bourne was one of the most celebrated of the Rectors of Minchinhampton. A son of Philip Bourne, of Worcestershire, he was elected Fellow of All Souls' in 1531. Ten years later he was made one of the first Prebendaries of Worcester, by Henry VIII; Archdeacon of Bedford, in 1549; Bishop of Bath and Wells in 1554, and Lord President of Wales. When Queen Elizabeth succeeded, he was deprived of his Bishopric for denying her supremacy, and died at Silverton, in Devonshire, where he is buried.

23. THOMAS TAYLOR, 1553. Appointed by William, Lord Windsor.

24. THOMAS FREEMAN, M.A., 1575. Appointed by Sir Henry Carey, of whom I know nothing.

25. GEORGE BYRCH, D.D., 1584. Appointed by John à Deane, whose burial is recorded in the parish registers : " John à Deane hujus Rectoriæ Firmarius, sepultus 1602." By this it is probably meant that he was patron of the living and not farmer of its revenues.

26. ANTHONY LAPTHORNE, D.D., 1612. Appointed by King James I. (pro hac vice). There is a well-known story of this Rector very much to his credit, which I transcribe from Wantner's MSS. History :—

" In the reigne of King James, one Mr Lapthorne was Minister of Minchinhampton, and Chapline in Ordinarie to ye King before named, who, being at Court, attending his duety, went one evening to see his Majesty and his nobles play at Bowles, where were many persons of Honour and quality, and amongst them, His Grace George Abbot, Lord Archbishop of Canterbury was one. Now it happened that whilst Mr Lapthorne was a spectator of their exercise, that the King laid a Bowle close to the Jack which ye Nobelman which bowled after ye King hit away, which put his Majesty into such a sudden passion that he began to swear at a most prodigious rate. Lapthorne, standing by and hearing the King strongly to sweare, expected every moment when ye Lord Archbishop would modestly have admonished the King not to swear ; but when he perceived that he took little or no notice thereof, Mr Lapthorne bouldly expressed himselfe as followeth (viz.), The King sweares, and the

Nobles will sweare, and if the Nobles sweare, the Commons they will sweare, and what a swearing Kingdom we shall have. And for you, my Lord Archbishop, that hath the immediate charge of his Majestie's soule, and to hear him swear and take God's sacred name in vaine, and to have never a word for God's sake, I will say to you as once Paul said to Ananias (though in another case), " Thou painted wall, God will smite thee." Which reasonable though rash reproof (saith my author) workt so great a Reformation in ye Court that if the King heard any man to swear he would bid them not to swear, for Lapthorne was comeing."

27. HENRY FOWLER, M.A., 1618. Appointed by Michael Halyday, probably descendant of Edward Haliday, whose brass, as already mentioned, is in Minchinhampton Church. There is a great deal to be said of this Rector, and the persecution he endured, which I must defer to another Chapter. He was assessed for " ship money " at £1 10s.

During the Commonwealth there were frequent " Intruders " in every parish where the Incumbent was opposed, or accused of being opposed, to the Puritans. I do not know how far these Intruders were officially appointed, but in many cases they turned the clergy out of their pulpits and churches, and even out of their houses. Walker, in his " Sufferings of the Clergy," gives a long list of Intruders in many parishes in Gloucestershire ; amongst others, two are mentioned at Minchinhampton, named respectively Doleman and Herne, and there is also a record of one Thomas Worden, the Intruder at Chipping Norton, and afterwards of Nailsworth, but I rather doubt whether Doleman was an intruder.

In all probability Fowler did not long survive the ill-treatment he received in 1643, but the registers during the Civil War and the Commonwealth are so defective that it is difficult to unravel some of the intricacies. For this reason I have no information of the date of Fowler's death, but the following note in the Register may help us a little :—

28. " WILLIAM DOLEMAN, Minister of Minchinhampton, died on the 8th day of April and was buried on the 12th day of April, 1649." Walker also mentions Doleman as having succeeded Fowler, and in connection with this Rector there is this curious entry in the Registers :—" Resolved upon the

question that all the glass of the windows and that all the doors, wainscots and benches that are left remaine a deed of gift to the parsonage house of Minchinhampton. Provided alwaies that if there come any claims or suite of law from any succeeding minister, or any other persons what-so-ever for dilapidations, that then this p'sent act be voyde to all intents and purposes as if it had never been made." This entry is signed " Will. Doleman."

29. SAMUEL HIERON or HEARN. This name occurs as Rector in the Lambeth MSS. in 1654 and 1655. Walker mentions him as an intruder, which he probably was, and he may have been ejected at the Restoration to make way for Dr Warmestree.

Samuel Clift, a Clothier of Avening was committed to Gloucester prison, charged with " maliciously molesting and interrupting Samuel Hearn" in the Church of Minchinhampton. The constable who arrested him set him in the Stocks ; and the Magistrate, who committed him, savagely struck him two or three blows, but upon his trial it came out that his only offence was that of standing silent in the Church with his hat on, and the Jury therefore acquitted him. The same Samuel Clift, with others, was also dragged from a meeting at Shortwood and taken to prison at Gloucester.

30. THOMAS WARMESTREE, D.D., 1660 ; also appointed by Michael Halyday. Dr. Warmestree was a student of Christ Church in 1624, and was created a D.D. in 1642. At the Restoration in 1660, he was appointed a Prebendary of Gloucester, and Rector of Minchinhampton, and subsequently Dean of Worcester. He was a prolific writer on Theological subjects, and he was evidently a Conformist, as, although the Act of Uniformity was passed during his incumbency of Minchinhampton, he continued to hold his preferments until his death.

31. JOHN FARRER, 1665. The living had now passed into the hands of the Sheppards, and this Rector was accordingly appointed by Philip Sheppard. He held the benefice for 52 years, the longest incumbency of any of the Rectors.

32. RALPH WILLETT, 1717. Appointed by Samuel Sheppard.

THE REV. WILLIAM COCKIN

33. PHILIP SHEPPARD, 1720. Appointed by his father, Samuel Sheppard. We have already given an account of this Rector's life.

34. ROBERT SALUSBURY HEATON, 1768. Appointed by Edward Sheppard, as mentioned in Ch. VII.

35. JOHN WHITE, D.D. Appointed by Edward Sheppard

36. HON. HARBOTTLE GRIMSTON, 1778. A member of the Verulam family. Appointed by Edward Sheppard.

37. HENRY CHARLES JEFFERIES, 1786. Also appointed by Edward Sheppard.

38. WILLIAM COCKIN, 1806. Appointed by Joseph Pitt. Numberless stories are told of this Rector. He was originally Curate both of Minchinhampton and Cherington, and after officiating at the former place, it is said, in top boots, he used to gallop off on his horse, which was waiting outside, to do duty at Cherington. There is a story of the manner in which he became Rector of Minchinhampton, which, if true, is perhaps not altogether to Mr Cockin's credit. Mr Joseph Pitt, solicitor, of Cirencester, either owned, or acted for the owner of the Advowson. On the Living becoming vacant in 1806, Mr Pitt expressed a doubt, in Mr Cockin's hearing, as to whom he should appoint, and, as the story goes, Cockin immediately said : " I bet you £1,000 you don't appoint me." The bet was taken and Cockin became Rector. There is a much pleasanter story of Mr Cockin, which, by the kindness of Miss Cockin, his great niece, I am able to give.

During his Curacy he became the owner of The Lammas, together with the rest of the Pinfold Estate, by the demise of the last two owners, who were elderly maiden ladies. The will of the Misses Pinfold was disputed on behalf of two minors who were next-of-kin, one of these being the late Mr Edward Pinfold Wesley, who lived to a very advanced age at Nailsworth. Mr Cockin won the suit, and the following extract from a speech by Thomas, Lord Erskine, who had been the defendant's counsel, gives the reason for the old ladies' bequest :—

" Two old maids in a country town, being quizzical in their dress and demeanour, were not infrequently the sport of the idle boys in the market place, and, being so beset on their way to Church, a young Curate, who had just been appointed there, reproved the urchins as he passed in his gown and cassock, and, offering an arm to each of the ladies, conducted them triumphantly into their pew near the pulpit. A great intimacy followed, and dying not long afterwards they left him all they had. The will was disputed, and when I rose in my place to establish it I related the story and said : ' Such, gentlemen of the jury, is the value of small courtesies. In my first speech here I was browbeaten by the Judge upon the Bench, and honest Jack Lee took my part. When he died he left me this bag, and I need not say how much I value it. It shall serve me while I live, and when I die I will be buried in it.' "

Mr Cockin continued to live at the Lammas, where he dispensed great hospitality to his friends and neighbours. His guests used to sit round the fire after dinner in high " beehive " chairs, some of which are still to be seen in the neighbourhood, each with a small table and a bottle of port beside him. Cockin died March 3rd, 1841, aged 75 years, leaving a large cellar of wine, the sale of which, together with his furniture and other effects, lasted 8 days, between May 11th and 21st. He was a very good natured, hospitable man, very charitable to the poor, and a great favourite with his parishioners, many of whom he used to rebuke by name in his sermons.

39. CHARLES WHATELY, 1841. Appointed by David Ricardo.

40. EDWARD COLNETT OLDFIELD, 1865. Appointed by Henry David Ricardo.

41. FRANK ALBERT MATHER, 1885. Appointed by Capt. H. G. Ricardo, R.A.

42. EDWARD LONSDALE BRYANS, 1896. Appointed by Major Ricardo.

43. FREDERICK DOUGLAS BATEMAN, 1912. Also appointed by Major Ricardo.

At the time of writing, the Rev. F. D. Bateman is about to resign the Incumbency, and the Rev. F. W. Sears, at present Vicar of Nailsworth, has been appointed in his stead by Lt.-Col. H. G. Ricardo, R.A. Mr Sears will therefore be the 44th Rector of Minchinhampton.

CHANTRY PRIESTS AT MINCHINHAMPTON

[1]Chantries existed in England as early as the 12th century. According to Dr Hook, even the sanction of the Bishop of the Diocese was not required for their foundation. They were set up under the general authority of the Pope. In the earliest period there were no restraints upon their endowment, but, after the passing of the Mortmain Acts, the King's license was required for the assignment of lands for the purpose.

Special Chapels, generally within the Church, but sometimes outside, were frequently erected by persons of wealth and rank to receive the Altars at which the Chantry, or " Singing Priests," officiated, praying for the souls of all the faithful departed in general, and those of the founder and his kin in particular. A special chapel was not necessary for the establishment of the Chantry, as these offices might be said at any of the Altars within the Church. Some of these Chantry Chapels were afterwards used as family burial places, and in the time of their glory were of exquisite design and workmanship, and formed beautiful additions to the Church buildings. Even now, notwithstanding the neglect from which they have for centuries suffered, they add greatly to the picturesque effect of the ancient Churches.

The relations which existed between the parochial clergy and the chantry priests are rather obscure. Where there were special chapels no difficulties would probably arise, but in cases in which they had to celebrate at the same altars, friction might easily take place.

The following are the only names of chantry priests which I have been able to discover :—

THOMAS DE CHALKFORD, presented in 1341 to the chantry of the Blessed Mary in the Church of Hampton Monialium, by William de Prestbury, Rector of the said Church. This appears to be the first priest appointed to officiate in this chantry after its foundation by William de Prestbury.

PETER AVENYNGE, appointed to the same chantry, 1348.

PETER DE ASHWELL appointed to the same chantry in 1349, by William de Prestbury. As we have seen, there was a great unrest amongst the Rectors in 1349, and apparently also amongst the chantry priests.

[1] Sir John Maclean in B. & G. Arch. Trans., Vol. VIII., p. 229.

PHILIP ARENA presented to the same chantry by John de Middleton, Rector of the Church of Hampton, also in 1349. This presentation is from the Register of the Priory of Woodchester, during the vacancy of the See (Sede vacante), folio 128.

GEOFFRY WYKE, probably appointed by Dr Richard Alkeryngton in 1405.

JOHN SMYTH, appointed in 1458, by William Gyan, rector to the " Chantry of the Blessed Mary in the cemetery of the Church of the Holy Trinity of Minchinhampton."

RICHARD GRAVENER, last chantry priest, pensioned about 1547. During that year, or perhaps rather earlier, a commission was appointed to enquire into the revenues of Chantries, and to recommend for pensions the priests who had ministered in them and had been left without means of subsistence, owing to the confiscations at the time of the Reformation. An inventory was also to be taken of all plate and jewels remaining, though this does not seem to have brought in much, either because portable valuables had already been confiscated, or had been hidden by the priests. The pensions do not seem to have erred on the side of generosity, though allowance must be made for the greater value of money at that time.

The following is the Certificate of the appointment of the Commission :—

" The Countie of Gloucetur with the Cities of Bristowe and Gloucetur.

The Certificat off Anthony Hungerforde Walter Bucler William Sharyngton & Milez Partridge knightes Arthure Porter Richarde Tracye Thomas Throckemerton Esquyers Thomas Sterneholde and Richard Pate Gentilmen Commyssioners appointed by vertue of the Kinge maiestiez Commyssion beringe the date xiiijth daye of ffebruarie in the Secounde yere of the reigne of Edwarde the Sixthe by the grace of godd kynge of Englonde ffraunce and Irelonde Defendo[r] of the faith and in this Churche of Englonde and also of Irelande supreme hedde vnto theym directed to take the Survey of all Colledges Chauntriez ffreechappelle and other like within the saied Countie and Cities as hereafter ensuythe."

The enquiries of the Commission seem to have been of a very exhaustive nature, and elaborate reports were drawn up.

The following relates to Minchinhampton, and to the chantry founded by William de Prestbury in 1338 :—

THE P'ISHE OF MINCHYNGHAMPTON within the deanery aforeseid [Stonehouse] where are of houseling people

V^c

Oure lady Chauntry.

ffounded by one Wiffm Prestbury & other & the land$_e$ putt in feoffm^t wth thissuez & $\text{p}$fitt$_e$ whereof there hath ben a pryest manteigned singing dayly at thalter of o^r lady in a Chapell situate wthin thep ishe Churche yard & ev̆y holyday to helpe to singe the dyvyne ȿuice in the Same Churche & to praye for the founders sowle & all x$\tilde{\text{p}}$en sowles.

Sr Richard Gravener Incūbent there of thage of lx yeres having no other lyving then in the seid ȿuice which is yerely - - - - - - - vj^{li}

The land$_e$ & teñt$_e$ belonging to the same are of the yerely value of - - - viij^{li} xvij^s iij^d ob̆ whereof

In rep^{t}sez yerely - - - - - xxv^s j^d ob̆

And so remayneth clere by yere - - vij^{li} xij^s ij^d

Ornament$_e$ plate and Juell$_e$ to the same - - noone

The foregoing extract shows that Prestbury's chantry was not within the Church, but outside in a chapel of its own. I have heard that at the Restoration in 1842 a pavement with many incised gravestones was discovered near the present west entrance, and this may have been the site of the chantry chapel. It is also quite possible that dame Alice Hampton's bell was given by her as a Sanctus Bell for the use of this Chapel, which, having been allowed to fall into decay, was pulled down. The bell was subsequently sold for the use of the second Market house, on the demolition of which it came into the possession of the writer's grandfather, as already stated.

There is also an entry by the Commissioners to some charity land at Avening, which appears to have been confiscated.

AVENYNGE

Obitte land$_e$ in the seid poche

To the yerelie value of - - - vj^s viij^d whereof

Distributed to the pore yerely - - - ij^s viij^d

CHAPTER XIV.

THE PERSECUTION OF THE
REV. HENRY FOWLER AND OTHER CLERGY
BY THE PURITANS

HENRY FOWLER became Rector of Minchinhampton in 1618. He was probably one of the Gloucestershire Fowlers, a branch of which family held the manor of Stonehouse for many generations. He had a son also named Henry, of whom Bigland, quoting Wood, says : " Henry Fowler, of Oriel College, who, after he had become a graduate, served very faithfully in his Majesty's Army during the grand Rebellion, and afterwards betook himself to the study of Physic, which he did with good success in his own country." He was quite a celebrated physician, and an alderman of Gloucester, and he also presented 14 valuable MSS. collected by him to the Cathedral College Library. He died March 16th, 1678.

It may be imagined that neither the father nor the son were likely to be looked on with favour by the Roundhead party, and they especially incurred the wrath of one Jeremy Buck, a captain in the Parliamentary Army. This man has a remarkable history. He was the son of a mercer, of Minchinhampton, of the same name, and was probably born about 1620. He married, March 11th, 1641, Ursula, eldest daughter of William Selwyn, of Matson, who was baptized at Stonehouse in 1632, and therefore as an adult, but I have no record of the date of her birth. The first mention of Jeremy Buck occurs in January, 1642, just before the investment and capture of Cirencester by Prince Rupert. He was serving as a captain in the Parliamentary army, and in a tract of the time appears this record, very little to his credit :—

"Captain Buck (a busie mercer, of Hampton Rode)[1] had a coward's wit with him, and that morning shifted himselfe out of the towne under pretence to fetch in more forces." By this dishonourable trick he escaped the dangers of the siege and subsequent pillage of the town.

The following account of his persecution of the Rev. Henry Fowler is taken from Walker's· "Sufferings of the Clergy," pp. 242-243, and appears to be transcribed from an earlier work, "Mercurius Rusticus, or the Countries Complaint" (London, 1685) :—

"I have no direct information of this sequestration, and only guess at it from the Greatness of his other Sufferings, which were these. On New Year's Day, 1643, a Party of Souldiers, sent by one Captain Buck, came to his House, and, finding him by the Fire, seized him as their Prisoner, and, though he readily submitted to them, yet one of them took him by the throat, and held the point of his Sword to his Breast ; two more presented their Pistols to him, another shook his Poll-Ax over his Head, and others beat him with their Poll-Axes, Railing at him for Reading Common Prayer, and His Majesty's Proclamation, calling him Mass-Priest, Rogue, Rascal, with other contumelious language, as "Sirrah, you can furnish the King with a Musquet, a Corslet, and a Light Horse, but thou old Knave, thou canst not find anything at all for the Parliament." He was at that time sixty-two years of age, and had a Lameness upon him in one of his Hips ; but without regard to either age or lameness, they fell on him again with their Poll-Axes, and beat him, and bruised him in such a Barbarous manner that they made him a very cripple, without all possibility of Recovering the use of his Limbs ; and to enhance the Inhumanity of this outrage, all this was done in the Presence of his Wife and Children, who, with bended knees, entreated mercy and Compassion for him ; but all in vain, for instead of that some of the kindred and Friends of Captain Buck, who had sent them on this errand, stood by, jeering, and clapt their hands for Joy. This most accursed treatment of poor old Mr Fowler, threw him into a Bleeding, which lasted six hours ; insomuch that he was not able to stand. The next day likewise he lost his Retentive Faculty, in which wretched condition he continued very near

[1] Bibliotheca Gloucestrensis, p. 164 (Minchinhampton is frequently referred to as Hampton Rode, or road, during the Civil War.)

a month. Nor was this all, for by the many contusions and knocks which he received on his Head with their Poll-Axes, he lost his Hearing, which was not for some time, if ever, perfectly recover'd. At the same time also they rifled his House, particularly his Study, and took away all that was of value and portable.

" This usage one would think would have satisfied the most invetrate Rancor and Malice in the World, but it seems that Captain Buck was not of that opinion : and therefore some months after he comes in person to Mr Fowler's house : breaks open the window of his Son's Study, who was a Physician ; enters the house that way, and destroyed several things of very great value in the way of Physick as extract of Pearl, Aurum Potabile, Confection of Amber, pearl in Boxes, Bezoar stone, Compound Waters, etc. Upon which one of Mr Fowler's daughters telling Buck that he might be ashamed to spoil such things : He presently called her ――― and knocked her down with his Poll-Ax ; and being risen again knocked her down a second time, and after that a third time, and would no doubt a Fourth, had she then been able to rise again. Upon which Mrs Fowler asking him if he thought 'twas possible for her to stand by and see her Child murdered, Buck presently, without any regard either to her age, or sex, caught her by the throat, knock'd her down ; and when down, kick's her, and trampl'd on her with his Feet. After which he and his Rabble plundered the House, and so departed. If this monstrous Barbarity exceeds Belief, let it be known that August 18, 1643, it was deposed upon oath before Sir Robert Heath, Lord Chief Justice of the King's-Bench."

Another outrage perpetrated by the same Jeremy Buck on the Rev. Humphrey Jasper, Vicar of South Cerney, is recorded by Walker.[1] This unfortunate man venturing to read the Common Prayer in his Church, was plundered of all that he possessed, and, " as he was going to Oxford for the security of his life, he was taken prisoner by the Parliament forces. After some time he made his escape to the city of Gloucester to a son he had there, a clergyman who entertained him privately, until Cirencester was taken by the King's forces, and, then coming home to South Cerney, he was forced to take strawricks and hayricks for his lodging. About which

―――――
[1] Walker's Sufferings of the Clergy ; p. 282.

time the Parliament soldiers took him prisoner again, and forced him to preach a sermon to a great number of their Officers and Soldiers with many of the Parishioners, but for all that he had so much courage as to speak in the pulpit against their Parliamentary Proceedings, and made a comparison that if Lucifer was in Heaven, he did not presume to sit in God's throne, but he thought the Devil was in the Parliament in sitting in the King's throne. Upon which the common soldiers would have killed him before he came out of the church had it not been for their officers. However, they guarded him to his own house, and afterwards brought him over to Cirencester, and Captain Buck, one of their officers, threatened to hang him on the King's Head sign post there, which would have been done if John George, Esq., and Col. Fettiplace had not got him out of their hands and sent him home under a guard." The foregoing account is signed by Humphrey Jasper, eldest son of the Vicar.

These outrages were by no means isolated cases ; on the contrary, almost every Royalist clergyman in England suffered persecution in a greater or less degree. In the neighbouring parish of Woodchester, the Rector, the Rev. John Feribee, was treated with great brutality, as the following account, also taken from Walker, will show :—

" Feribee, John—He was Rector of Woodchester, in Gloucestershire, and, as he was one day at the Font, a party of Massy's soldiers came in with drawn swords, pulled off his surplice (which one of them, putting on, wore on his way back), tore the Common Prayer Book, stript him of all his clothes, except a pair of drawers, and drove him (with many others) bare-footed and bare-legged, thro' thick and thin, in cold, wet and dirty ways, and weather, prisoners into Gloucester, where they were kept for many days in a damp low room under the College School, without a fire. Three daughters of one Mr Portlock, of Cirencester, hearing of his misery, made up a sum of money to Ransome him, which they sent by one J. Greenway, a Parliament soldier (and a kinsman to them) who had the conscience to keep every farthing to himself. This Greenway was a poor butcher, but by plundering had gotten a considerable estate, which after wasted as fast as he had got it, and his children wanted before they died."

Jeremy Buck had nothing to do with the latter outrage, as the scene of his activities was in other parts of the County, and, moreover, he does not appear to have served in the Parliamentary army during the siege of Gloucester. It seems strange that a man of his character, and a Roundhead too, should have married into so aristocratic a Royalist family as the Selwyns, of Matson, one of whom, Jeremy Buck's father-in-law, entertained Charles I. with his sons, Charles and James, at Matson House, for twenty-six days, during the abortive attempt to capture Gloucester in August and the early part of September, 1643. After his marriage, Jeremy Buck blossomed out as an Esquire, with a coat of arms containing three bucks-heads, which he impaled with those of Selwyn ; probably, like many others, he enriched himself by plunder taken from the Royalists, which enabled him to purchase this honour. There is the following inscription in Minchin-hampton Church on a tablet in memory of Jeremy Buck, under the Arms impaled as above :—

Piae Memoriæ Jeremiæ Bucke.
Arm. qui cum 35 soles.
Enumeravit fato correptus prœpropero[1]
die Dominico ante Nativitatem Christi
Vitam cum Morte commutavit
Mæstissima conjux Ursula Bucke
Hoc Marmor erigi curavit.

Jeremy Buck had a son and two daughters by Ursula. The son and eldest daughter died unmarried, and only the younger daughter married. All three, together with their father, are buried at Minchinhampton. The name is spelt Bucke in the epitaph, but in all the other memorials, including Jeremy's father's, the name is spelt " Buck."

Whatever Jeremy Buck's character may have been, there is nothing but good to be said of Ursula, who seems to have been a most devoted wife and mother, though it is strange that her influence, coming as she did from a Royalist family, was not sufficient to deter her husband from his more violent acts, which occurred after their marriage. A few years subsequent to Jeremy Buck's death, Ursula married Thomas Tooke, of Elmestree, near Tetbury, whom she survived. She appears to have come back to Minchinhampton after the

---

[1] So given in Bigland. The word is now illegible.

death of her second husband, as three of her children by him are buried there. Tooke is buried at Tetbury, where there is a monument to him, but I cannot trace the date of Ursula's death or the place of her burial. She left some charities, which are thus recorded :—

" Mrs Ursula Tooke, of this town in the year 1698 (as well at the request of her son Jeremy Buck, Gent., as of her own charitable inclination), settled lands in trust, by estimation, twenty acres in the west field of Minchinhampton, and gave eighty pounds for improving the same, for the following uses for ever, to wit, 40 shillings a year to be paid to the Trustees, their Heirs and assigns, for their care in the said trust, eight pounds for keeping at school six boys, and finding them books, and £5 yearly to four poor people. If the rent of the said lands should exceed or fall short of 15 pounds per annum, a proportionable addition or abatement is to be made in the schoolmaster's salary, and in the annuities to the poor people."

The request of Jeremy Buck, junior, must have remained in abeyance during Ursula's Marriage to Thomas Tooke, as he died May 2nd, 1668, and his death is thus recorded on his tomb-stone :—

To the happy Memorie of
Jeremiah Buck, Batchelor,
the eldest son of
Jeremiah Buck, Esq.,
And of Ursula, his wife,
Who died May 2nd, 1668.

The bequest, therefore, was not made until 30 years after the death of Jeremiah Buck, junior. This charity at the present time produces £30 p. annum, but I have never heard of the Trustees claiming 40s p. annum for their care of the Trust. The income is now devoted to the payment of annuities of 4 guineas each to four poor widows, and the balance is merged in the Minchinhampton Educational Foundation.

Ursula's receipt for " Plumb pudding " is still in existence, and those who have used it say that it is a very good one.

CHAPTER XV.

AVENING CHURCH

IT is fortunate that Avening Church escaped the ruthless restoration inflicted on the sister Church at Minchinhampton, and that it was left unrestored to a time when ancient Church architecture and archæology were better understood and appreciated. Thus one of the most interesting churches in the County has been preserved for us ; and though some mutilations have occurred during the eight centuries which have passed since its foundation, much of the ancient structure still remains, and now that incongruities have been swept away, and the fabric reverently restored, it stands as a beautiful and, let us hope, lasting monument of ancient church architecture.

There is no evidence of a church having existed at Avening in Saxon times, and, if there was one, all trace of it has disappeared. There is also no authentic record of the date of the building of the earlier Norman part of the present church, nor have I as yet been able to discover the date of its consecration and dedication to the Holy Rood, or Cross, but it was probably erected towards the end of the 11th century, or the beginning of the 12th. The remains of the ancient Norman Church, which still exist, bear the easily recognised family resemblance to those which are still to be seen in this County and in Normandy, though in the latter there is usually evidence of a refinement of detail and enrichment which marks the French workman as compared with his English neighbour. In each case we see the same massive walls, pierced by small round-headed windows without mullions, deeply recessed and splayed inwards, arcades and doorways with bold semicircular arches and large and simple mouldings, or decorated

AVENING CHURCH (EXTERIOR)

with the characteristic chevron or other ornaments ; very flat buttresses, if any at all, and a general solidity and grandeur of structure which belongs to no other style of mediæval architecture.

The Church, however, as it now stands, is of many dates, the original having been altered and added to at various times. It is cruciform in plan, and consists of a nave 42′ × 22′, with a shallow aisle on the north side and a north porch ; a tower in the centre of the Church, with a north transept 16′ 6″ × 21′, and a south transept 18′ × 13′ 6″, a chancel 33′ × 16′ 6″, and from indications which still remain there was a small chapel, perhaps a Lady chapel, in the angle formed by the junction of the chancel and the north transept. On the site of this chapel a piscina still exists outside the northern wall of the chancel ; the eastern foundations of this chapel can also be traced. Some tiles and other relics were found on the spot, and a piece of molten metal, from which it is inferred that the chapel was possibly destroyed by fire.

We may now endeavour to trace the successive alterations and additions to the Church, and the time at which they were probably made.

The Norman church, a great part of which still remains, consisted, so far as we can see from the existing walls, of a nave with north and south doorways and an arcade of two arches opening into a short narrow aisle or chapel. There was a tower between the nave and chancel, having a groined roof, with arches on the east and west sides towards the chancel and nave, and windows high up on the north and south sides. There was also a chancel with groined roof, the eastern wall of which has been removed, and, consequently, there is now no evidence on which we can form an opinion as to whether the chancel had an apse or square end ; the former was usual in Normandy, but less common in England.

In this Norman edifice numerous alterations were made in the 13th, 14th, and 15th centuries, and probably in the following order :—

To the nave was added the present north aisle, and to the tower two transepts, with arches constructed in the old Norman walls of the tower, giving access to them. To this period also probably belongs the small north chapel mentioned above, opening into the chancel by a doorway, the jambs of which

are still to be seen.   At a later date were added the eastern
and western windows.   The next important change was the
addition of the eastern bay of the chancel, a work of great
artistic merit.   It is groined in stone, and the vaulting ribs are
so arranged as to harmonise with the lines and proportions of
the earlier vault.   The piscina still remains, and, though
mutilated, it was originally a feature of great beauty, and
perhaps some of the fragments of the beautiful stone carving
found under the flooring of the Church at its restoration may
have formed part of this.   The object of this extension of the
chancel is not certain, but Mr Carpenter suggests that it was
perhaps to provide a Lady Chapel in place of the one on the
north side, said to have been burnt down.

At a rather later date, and probably in the 14th century,
two of the southern windows of the nave were inserted, as well
as the beautiful northern and eastern windows of the north
transept.   To this period also belong the fine timber roof of
the nave and the buttresses against the south wall, which shews
signs of having inclined outwards.   Lastly, the upper stage
and battlements of the tower were added, and also the parvise
over the north porch.   The floor of the parvise has now been
removed to shew the beautiful head of the Norman doorway.
The west wall of the nave above the ancient door is of modern
construction.   It is said that the old west window was blown
in during service in the early part of the 19th century, and the
present two-light round-headed window was then erected in
its place.

[1]" The porch is of two dates.   When constructed in the
13th century it had only one story, the roof of which was clear
of the Norman door on the north side ; but in the 15th century
it was divided into two stories, the upper one serving as a
parvise or porch, and probably also as a priest's lodging.   The
Norman arch fortunately survived all the many restorations,
and is of great beauty and interest.   The capitals, which rest
on twisted shafts, are carved on the east side with two lions,
which appear to merge into a grotesque human face."   The
access to the priest's lodging was probably a low archway, still
there, and a communication may have existed to this doorway
from the rood loft stairs by a floor, which probably existed
over the north aisle.

[1] Rev. Canon Bazeley in B. & G. Trans., Vol. XXII, p. 15.

AVENING CHURCH (INTERIOR)

On entering the Church, two curious carvings are to be seen built into the wall. Dr. Fryer says of these fragments :—
[1]" Two fragments belonging to a Norman font are built into the ancient Church at Avening. One small, sadly mutilated fragment (7" × 7") indicates that it once formed a fraction of a rectangular stone font ornamented with a round-headed arch, supported by a pillar and a wall bracket. The larger part of this rectangular bowl is in the north wall of the nave, and forms part of the internal jamb of the north door. This fragment is sufficiently large (2' 2½" × 1' 1¾") to show that the bowl was originally 2¾ feet in length. The Avening font has an arcade of rudely cut, round-headed arches, supported alternately on pillars and wall brackets, containing three pairs of figures. Five figures still remain, and one circular pillar, supporting the arcade, has its capital and base. The apostles were so frequently sculptured on Norman fonts that it is probable the bowl at Avening had six apostles on the one side and six on the other, while the two other faces would doubtless be ornamented in some other way."

Avening church was fortunate in having for its restorer so eminent an architect as the late Mr Micklethwaite, who preserved all its ancient features, where possible, and inserted no new work unless it was absolutely necessary for the security of the building. A most unfortunate accident happened during the restoration. The foundations of the tower and of the south wall of the nave, together with the buttresses, had been excavated and securely underpinned, and the workmen were engaged in making equally secure the centre pillar of the north aisle arcade, when, without warning, the pillar slid into an open vault beneath the floor of the aisle, and fell down, bringing with it a great part of the nave and the north aisle, the workmen being barely able to escape without injury. It was fortunate indeed that so much underpinning had been done, otherwise, in Mr Micklethwaite's opinion, the tower would have fallen and the Church would have become a heap of ruins. As it was, the loss occasioned a further expenditure of about £500, which the building committee had to raise.

There is a quaint Commonwealth table, formerly used as a Communion table in the chancel, and now dedicated to the

[1] Trans. B. & G. Arch. Soc., Vol. XXXIV, pp 196-7

same purpose, on the site of the ancient parish altar, bearing
this inscription :—

> Holiness unto the Lord
> Hallelujah Salvacion and Glory
> J. 1657 R.
> T. 1657 W.
> Giles Whiting

There are the remains of another altar, also decorated
with the Chevron, in a similar position on the opposite side
of the nave.

The Avening bells originally numbered five. One is
by Abraham Rudhall, inscribed " Prosperity to this Parish,
1756." Three are dated Anno Domini 1628, and one with
no date.

About 1830 the treble bell at Cherington was stolen and
set up in Avening tower to make a ring of six. A vulgar
error prevailed in the locality that if a bell could be taken from
one tower, and put in another without the thieves being
caught in the act, there was no redress. This was not the
view taken by the Judge when the case was tried at the assizes,
and all implicated in the theft sentenced to six months
hard labour. Some local ballads on the subject are still
remembered in Avening.

Monuments Within the Church

In the south transept are some elaborate monuments to
the Driver family, who owned the estates of Aston and Lowesmoor, reputed manors within the manor of Avening, for
several generations. John Driver died in 1681, aged 85,
and his wife in 1675, aged 73. Charles, their son, died in 1696,
aged five years, and the second son, Matthew, who was a Fellow
of All Souls College, Oxford, also died in 1661, aged 27. Thereupon the estate devolved upon the third son, John, who died
in 1687, aged 51, to whom there is a very florid monumental
effigy depicting a bewigged man, holding a civic crown in one
hand and the other resting upon a skull. There is also an
inscription in Latin and Greek, attributing many virtues to
him, and recording that the monument was erected by his widow
Elizabeth at her own cost. There are many more inscriptions on flat stones to members of the Driver family, the
widow of the last of whom sold Aston to one Beresford, who

resold it to the Estcourts of Estcourt House, and Losemoor to the Slopers, of Tetbury. Both estates were subsequently bought by Mr Lowsley, whose great grandson, Mr Geo. Lowsley Williams, of Chavenage, is the present owner, both of Aston and Losemoor.

There is also a monument to Dr Browne, who bought Avening Court from the Sheppards, and at his death it was bought by William Playne, senior.

By far the most remarkable monument in Avening Church is that to Henry Brydges, in the north aisle. It represents a man kneeling on a cushion in the attitude of prayer. He is partly dressed in armour, and wears long hair and beard. Below is the following inscription :—

> " Here lyeth the body of Henry Brydges
> Esquoir son to John Lord Chandos
> Baron of Shewdley who departed this life
> the 24th day of Januari Anno Dom. 1615."

There are many local traditions connected with this Henry Brydges. He is said to have lived at the house now called the Church Farm, though I think it is more likely that he lived at Avening Court, and to have been a notorious highwayman ; and there are stories of horses shod hind before. and of the terror which he created in the whole countryside, Mrs Dent[1] (Annals of Winchcombe and Sudeley, p. 214) says : " Henry the fourth son of the first Lord Chandos of Sudeley, according to his father's will, must have been left with very slender means ; and having in those times of peace no vent for his love of adventure, he is said to have followed the life of a freebooter, indulging in deeds of lawlessness and robbery almost surpassing our modern powers of belief. We can readily imagine how the almost impassable roads, thick woods, and broken ground of this neighbourhood must have aided the young nobleman in his first steps as a freebooter." Besides being a highwayman, Henry Brydges was also a pirate, as the following extract will show :—

1611. James I. granted to Henry Brydges, of Avening, County of Gloucester, a pardon for piracy, which is recorded in these words. "And whereas Henry Brydges, formerly of

---

[1] Mrs Dent says he married the eldest daughter of Samuel Sheppard of Avening. This is manifestly an error, as Samuel Sheppard was a boy of thirteen at the time of the death of Henry Brydges, and did not acquire the Avening estate till 1651. Moreover, both his daughters died in infancy.

Avening, in the County of Gloucester, and others on the 20th day of February, in the 23rd year of the reign of Her Majesty Elizabeth, late Queen of England, France, and Ireland, did arm and supply with gunpowder, picks, darts and other weapons of warlike nature, the aforesaid ships called the Salamander, of the port of Bristol, and the Mary Grace, of Penzance, on the coast of Cornwall, and did feloniously send the same to sea, and support, aid, and abet John Kirkham and Thomas Maid, the respective captains and others their accomplices and associates, in perpetrating piracy on the aforesaid ship the Whalefishe and its cargo of salt, hemp, and coined metal. Know all men that we by our clemency by this our word of grace spoken and exercised, and by this our act, do pardon, remit, relax and condone and forgive the said Henry Brydges, formerly of Avening, in the county of Gloucester, Merchant." The Whalefishe was a Danish ship belonging to Copenhagen, and the privateers took from it a quantity of salt valued at £30, some flax, and £90 in Spanish coin. Severin Severeinson, described as "the guardian under God and Captain of the Whalefishe," went back to his home at Elsinore, and set the law in motion against Brydges and his captains. What happened to the latter is not stated, but Henry Brydges was pardoned and bound over to "keep the peace of Parliament of 10 Edward III." After this, Brydges appears to have retired to Avening and to have died there, and we may hope from the pious position in which he is depicted on the monument that he repented in his older years of the evil deeds of his youth.

He is believed to have married, perhaps late in life, Alice, widow of Walter Compton, of the same family as the Comptons, of Hartpury, in this County, a branch of which family lived for some time in the neighbourhood of Avening.

In connection with Walter and Alice Compton, a very curious action was brought, in the Consistory Court of Gloucester, in the year 1551. The details are of such a nature that they cannot be given in full, and the following are extracts from the official reports.

GLOUCESTER CONSISTORY COURT 1551 AVENING

Walter Compton v. Alice Compton, his wife. Divorce Nov. 12. Walter exhibited certain articles. Alice prayed restitution of conjugal rights.

Walter produced as witnesses Anne Halyday, Sybil Fyld, and Alice Beene, who were sworn, etc.

Edith Shrove was excommunicated for contumacy in not appearing, and decreed to be cited for Nov. 28th.

Nov. 28. Walter produced Adam Parkins and Edith Shrove. Deposition of witnesses on the part of Walter Compton.

"Anne Halyday aged 42 years of Bisselege (Bisley), where she had lived 23 years, had known the parties 18 years and being examined what displeasure, variaunce, strife or dispute was to this deponent's knowledge rysen betwixt the said parties, she answerethe that upon a Monedaye about eight or nine years agoe, the said Alice Compton sent for this deponent to come to her to a certain Myll of the said Walter Compton whereunto this deponent came, and there the said Alice said : "Alas that ever I was borne, for I am used as no woman ys, and rather than I will lyve this lyfe he shall rydde me or I will rydde hym . . ." This deponent counselled the same Alice to goe home agayne to her husband and to obey hym. The same Alice is and hath been of honest lyving in all thynges saving her tonge which she would suffer to go at large.

As touching the article that said Alice should beyre herself bold upon Sir Giles Poole,[1] she knoweth nothynge therein but she saith there hathe been communication that Sir Gieles should send Alice a bracelet . . . ."
She cannot say whether Alice left her husband of her own mind, or whether he put her away. As regards the demeanor of said Alice with (as it is supposed) one William Potter she knows nothing."

The other witnesses gave similar evidence, all speaking of Alice's unruly tongue. One Adam Parkins says :—

" There was often strife betwixt them, the more pitie. About Christmas 7 years agoe he was playing at tables with said Alice in her hall, and she said if her husband wold use himself as he had done she wold washe her handes in his hert bloud, affirming the same with

---

[1] Sir Giles Pool lived at Sapperton in the Manor House close to the Church. A descendant sold the property to the father ot Sir Robert Atkyns the Historian of the County. The House is now pulled down.

othes in the presence of her maydenes . . . He had
often heard said Alice say she would cause her brother
to break his Mazer[1] at his Court gates.   He had heard
her say she had lever keep Sir Gieles Poole's hounds
and hawks than to be Walter Compton's wife, and that
Walter Compton was a lustie child but Sir Gieles was
frowlicker and confessed she had a brachlet with gold
of the said Sir Gieles Poole."

Finally, on the 31st of December, the following judgment
was given, in which the judge seems anxious to accommodate
matters by giving neither party much advantage over the
other.

" Because Walter proved by witnesses the cruelty
of Alice the Judge pronounced for Walter as far as by law
he might, but finally pronounced such cruelty not to be
of such bitterness that he ought to divorce Walter from
Alice.   In like manner he pronounced the other allegations
of Walter not to be effectually proved so that the restitution prayed by Alice ought not to be.   Finally he restored
Walter to Alice, having first required of Alice sufficient
security to indemnify Walter if he required it, who then
prayed for security.   The Judge enjoyned Walter to
provide sufficient alimony and to pay Alice 5s 10d in
cash weekly, until such security be given by Alice."

I regret to say that the Judge's well-meant efforts to
accommodate the matrimonial difficulties of Walter and Alice
were not altogether effectual, as on June 28th of the following
year, we find Alice bringing another action to force Walter
to adhere to the terms of the judgment given.

It may readily be imagined that much of the evidence in
the above case is not fit for publication, but I have thought
that these extracts may not be uninteresting as illustrative of
some manners of the time.

[1] Mazer or Mazzard means the head.

CHAPTER XVI.

RECTORS OF AVENING

THE following is a list of the Rectors of Avening so far as I have been able to trace them. Probably before the appearance of the Rectors the services were conducted in the newly-erected Churches both in Avening and in Minchinhampton, by priests appointed and maintained by the Abbess of Caen. This was at the time a very common practice, and the priests so appointed were called " Vicars," though that name acquired a totally different signification after the Reformation :—

1. WILLIAM DE MONTFORT was living in 1291. He is described in the Papal Registers as Papal Chaplain, and Dean of S. Paul's, London. " He by indult of Alexander IV. (Rinaldo) held benefices to the amount of 300 marks, namely, the churches of Stratford, Avenynge and Whitchurch, in the Diocese of Worcester, Estrude in that of Winchester, Flikesburg in that of Lincoln, Dunet and Aldetheleye in that of Coventry and Lichfield, Angerham in that of Durham, and Colerne in that of Salisbury, prebends in London, Lichfield and Hereford, and a portion in Ledbury of that Diocese. He is now allowed to retain the same and to hold others to the total value of £300." This was a large sum in those days, and William de Montfort was not Papal Chaplain for nothing. Whether he kept curates at these places or did any duty himself is not stated.

2. PETER DOUCET.—Appointed October 7th, 1294, by Edward I., who held the temporalities of the Abbey of Caen for the usual reason. " There is a licence from William Ginsborough, Bishop of Worcester, to Peter, Rector of the Church of Avening, priest, to study within the Kingdom of

England, or without, from the present date (March, 1304) for 3 years." What became of the spiritualities of the people of Avening during these absences ?

There seems to have been a difficulty about the institution of Peter, as there is this entry in the Worcester Registers :—

> "A.D. 1294, Induction of Peter Doucet, Acolyte, treasurer of the Lady Mary, daughter of the King and a Nun of Ambersbury, by his Proctor, John Beyton, to the Church of Avening. And he was not instituted because he was absent and not in Holy Orders."

This difficulty seems to have been overcome in 1297, as there is this order to Godfrey Gifford, Bishop of Worcester. " Order to restore to Master Peter Doucet, the Church of Avenynge, which the Bishop took into the King's hands by virtue of the Kng's order to take into his hands the benefices of Alien secular parsons, whether they be Canons or Rectors of churches, or otherwise beneficed in the realm, of the power of the King of France and his adherents, because Peter is an alien, and the King wishes to show him favour for his long and good services to Eleanor, late Queen of England, the King's mother, and afterwards to Mary his daughter, a Nun of Ambersbury."

3. WILLIAM DE LEOBURY.—Appointed by Edward II., May 17th, 1325. " July 26th, 1325. Protection till Christmas for the Bishop of Winchester going beyond the sea on the King's service. Protection for the same time for the following going with the said Bishop :—William de Leobury, of the Church of Avenynge."

4. WILLIAM DE WYGORNIA.—Mentioned as late Rector in 1340 (Close Rolls.)

5. PHILIP BONVALET.—Was Proctor in England of the Abbess of Caen, and was appointed by Edward III. to the custody of all lands and goods of the Abbey in England taken into the King's hands during wars. Bonvalet was an alien by birth, " born of the Power of France," and by a " Pardon " dated September 1st, 1339, he is allowed to retain the Rectory of Avenynge on payment of a Moiety of the Taxation of the Church, amounting to 25 Marks per annum. This Rector appears to have been perpetually in hot water, as there are numerous Orders, Pardons and Directions not to intermeddle.

On Dec. 16th, 1347, a commission is appointed, consisting of Simon Borrett, Walter de Cirencestre, and William de Cheltenham, " To make inquiries touching a petition of Thomas, son and heir of John de Harstone, that whereas Philip Bonvalet, Proctor in England of the Abbess of Caen, unjustly ejected his father from a messuage, and half a virgate of land, whereof he was seized, and held the same to the use of the said Abbess until they were taken into the King's hands with the lands of the alien religious. The King will cause restitution to be made to him of the messuage and land, and to certify the King as to the truth of the statements made in the petition, and whether the premises are of ancient demesne or held at common law, and by what service. The Inquisition is to be taken in the presence of the Attorney, Maud, Countess of Ulster, to whom the King has committed the custody of the money, or Henry Earl of Lancaster, his brother."

I have no information as to whether restitution was made to Thomas de Harstone, but apparently the Abbess was satisfied with her Proctor, as there is this entry under date, Feb. 20th, 1361. " Georgia, Abbess of the Holy Trinity in Normandy, who lately came to England to further some business of hers there, and is about to go back, has given letters nominating Philip Bonvalet and Master Roger Mabon, as her Attornies in England for three years."

6. JOHN ERCHEBAND.—Leaves in exchange in 1373.

7. NICHOLAS MORIN.—Appointed by Richard II. in 1373.

8. WILLIAM DE BRITBY.—Appointed by Henry IV. in 1408.

9. JOHN TIMBRELL.—Presented in 1413, probably by Abbess of Caen.

10. NICHOLAS STURGION.—Presented in the same year.

11. JOHN LOCKHAWE.—Presented in 1416, probably by Henry V.

12. JOHN BROCKHOLES.—Presented in 1438, by Henry VI.

13. EDWARD WAGHORN.—Was Rector in 1498. Sir John Whitehead is mentioned as Chaplain, and Richard Ball and Thomas Hathway as Churchwardens.

14.—THOMAS TROWELL.—Rector in 1540. John Giles is mentioned as his parish priest.

15. STEVEN SAGAR.—Rector in 1542.

16. GILES COXE.—Died 1557.

17. EGEDIUS COKE.—Probably appointed by Lord Windsor on the death of Giles Cox. Egedius appears to have held the Living for a very short time, as he died the year after his appointment.

The Avening Registers begin 1557 and the first few pages are all signed at the bottom William Bushe, Rector, showing that they are a copy of some former entries either in a book or on loose pages.

Under " Buringe," 1558, comes the entry " Egedius Coke Rector obiit xxx Augustii." This Latin form of the Christian name Giles appears in the registers twice in christenings in 1567 ; in one wedding in 1558, and a christening in 1564 ; twice in 1563, and once in 1568.

18 WILLIAM INMAN.—Appointed by Edward Lord Windsor, instituted 1558.

19. GILES SANSOME.—Appointed by Lord Windsor. Instituted 1577.

20. WILLIAM BUSHE.—Probably appointed by Lord Windsor. According to the Avening Register he died Dec. 1st, 1609. Buried at Avening.

21. WILLIAM HALL.—Appointed by Henry Pigott and John Hall. Instituted in 1609.

22. CHARLES DEANE.—Appointed by William Umfreville, by assignment of a grant from Lord Windsor. Assessed for Ship Money at £1 16s.

23. WILLIAM HALL.—Instituted 1642. Appointed by Charles I. " pro hac vice." He was probably a son of the above mentioned Rector of the same name. He declared against the Act of Uniformity, but afterwards conformed, and therefore was not ejected from the living. He died Nov. 9th, 1683.

24. ROBERT FRAMPTON.—Appointed by Philip Sheppard. Instituted 1684. This is one of the most celebrated of the Avening Rectors, though he held the living for a very short

time. He held also some living in Dorsetshire which, at the earnest request of his friend Philip Sheppard, he changed with that of Avening, which he held " in commendam," in order that he might have some place of retirement within the Diocese of Gloucester, to which he had been appointed as Bishop in 1680 ; but, finding the Rectory House in a ruinous condition, he left it in the following year, and took instead the Vicarage of Standish, just then vacant, and in the gift of the Bishop of Gloucester.

Dr. Frampton was one of the seven Bishops who, headed by Sancroft, Archbishop of Canterbury, refused to obey the order of James II. that the " Declaration of Indulgence " should be read on two successive Sundays in every Church within each Diocese in the Kingdom. The Archbishop and six of the Bishops met at Lambeth Palace to draw up a protest against the Order, which they did in a very temperate letter, declining to publish the Declaration, which they considered to be illegal, and against which they had consistently preached. But it happened that Frampton was half an hour late at this meeting, having been detained in his diocese. The Archbishop urged them to wait for him, saying : " I am sure our brother of Gloucester with his black mare is on the gallop." The other bishops, however, decided not to wait, and over persuaded the reluctant Archbishop, who had a great affection for Frampton, and they accordingly then presented their protest to the King. James was furious, and committed all the seven Bishops to the Tower. The whole population turned out in their honour, and their going into captivity was like a triumphal progress. Frampton was anxious to present his protest alone, but he was dissuaded by the Archbishop, who said : " Brother, there will come a time when your constancy and courage may do the Church more service." Though not in confinement, Frampton spent most of his time at the Tower, and on leaving at night, multitudes thronged his coach asking for his blessing. Amongst those sent to the Tower was Sir Jonathan Trelawny, Bishop of Bristol, the hero of the Cornish song with the well-known refrain :—

> And have they fixed the where and when,
> And shall Trelawny die ?
> There's twenty thousand Cornish men
> Will know the reason why.

At length, on the 29th of June, the seven appeared before the Court of King's Bench, and, although the Jury had been picked and the Judges were creatures of James, the attitude of the populace was so threatening that they pronounced a verdict of Not Guilty, amidst a roar of applause.

But a still more serious crisis arose for the Church, and Dr. Frampton was one of the seven Bishops who refused to take the oath of allegiance to William III., known as the " Nonjuring Bishops," his old friend Archbishop Sancroft, being also of the number.

Everyone holding any ecclesiastical or academic preferment was ordered to take the oath by the first of August, 1689. Six months were allowed for reconsideration ; but if, on the first of February, 1690, he still refused, sentence of deprivation was passed, and Frampton, who stoutly refused to take the oath, was deprived of his Bishopric on February 1st, 1690. He continued to be Vicar of Standish, apparently by tacit consent, and at any rate he held it till his death, though after paying all charges it was only worth £40 a year. He had previously rebuilt the Parsonage House, and the late Archdeacon Sheringham, when Vicar of Standish, wrote : " I hold myself fortunate in occupying the house which once held the brave old Bishop who sacrificed his place to his conscience, and died here in peace, and full of years."

Frampton was a very celebrated preacher, even in early life. Pepys speaks of him as " a young man of a mighty ready tongue, preaching the most like an apostle that ever I heard man ; it was much the best time that I ever spent in my life at Church."

And Evelyn says: " That famous Preacher, Dr. Frampton, not only a very pious and holy man, but excellent in the Pulpit for the moving affections."

A Life of Frampton was written soon after his death, and this has been edited and published by Rev. T. S. Evans. The Editor, in the Preface to the Life, says : " In his honesty, his sense of humour, his generosity, his personal bravery, his readiness in moments of danger, his eagerness to aid the suffering and the oppressed, in his broad charity and by his abiding sense of duty to a higher than human law, Robert Frampton is an Englishman of the best type."

Frampton had been a great traveller in Palestine and the East, and there is said to be a portrait of him, bronzed by the sun, in the Palace at Gloucester.

Wantner says of him : " The Right Reverend Father in God, Doctor Robert Frampton, Lord Bishop of Gloucester (who hath been a very great Traviler) did say in my hearing that the Tower (of Minchinhampton) did much resemble the Pillar erected in memory of Absolon, ye son of ye Kingly Prophet David." But there is only a faint resemblance between the so-called Tower of Absalom and that of Minchinhampton Church.

Frampton died in June, 1708, aged 86. He would never acknowledge that he had been rightfully deprived of his Bishopric, nor would he ever read the prayer for the King's Majesty. He is buried in Standish Church, and there is this inscription on his Tomb :—

ROBERTUS FRAMPTON

Episcopus Glocestrensis
Cætera quis nescit ?
Obiit
VIII. Calend : Junii

Anno $\left\{ \begin{array}{l} \text{Ætatis 86} \\ \text{Consecrationis 28} \\ \text{Æræ Christianæ 1708} \end{array} \right.$

Thus, though he only held the emoluments of the Bishopric for 10 years, he always considered that he had been Bishop till the end of his life—a period of 28 years.

Frampton married in 1687, Mrs Mary Canning, who lies buried in the Lady Chapel of Gloucester Cathedral, and the following inscription is on the tomb :—

" M. S. Fæminæ inter optimas numerandæ, dominæ Mariæ Frampton, quæ vitam sancte actam suavissima in Xto morte consummavit, Octr. 11, 1680."

He also had a daughter, whose devoted affection was a great comfort to her father in his adversity.

25. GEORGE BULL, D.D.—Appointed by Philip Sheppard. Instituted, 1685. This was also a very celebrated Rector, who afterwards became Bishop of St. David's, but I must

defer a sketch of his life for the present in order to finish the list of the Rectors.

26. JOHN SWYNFEN.—Appointed by Queen Anne, " pro hac vice." Instituted, 1705. It is recorded that when Dr. Frampton vacated the Living of Avening, he left it at the disposal of the proper Patron, Philip Sheppard, but " Doctor Bull was not so kind to his Patron, for when raised to the See of St. David's, he left the Living to the disposal of the Crown ; " and hence the appointment of this Rector by Queen Anne. I do not know by what law Dr. Bull was enabled to do this, but probably a gift to the Crown took precedence of everything else. Swinfen also held the Living of Beverston with that of Avening, and, when residing at the former place, he required the Avening people to come over to him when they desired his services, and for this reason many of the Avening marriages are recorded in the Beverston registers. Swinfen died April 29th, 1728, and is buried at Avening.

27. PHILIP SHEPPARD.—Was instituted 1728, and is said in the Gloucester Diocesan Records to have been appointed by William Sanford. This is probably a mistake, as the Advowson of the Living of Avening undoubtedly belonged to Samuel Sheppard the elder, who dealt with it by settlement in favour of his younger son, Edward, as stated above, and there would not appear to have been any object in selling the next presentation, as it would be natural that it would be given by Samuel to his son when vacant.

28. ROBERT SALUSBURY HEATON.—Instituted, 1769. Appointed by Thomas Gryffin and Edmund Clutterbuck, the Trustees who held the purchase money for the next presentation to the Livings of Minchinhampton and Avening as mentioned in Chapter VII.

29. THOMAS CHAMBERLAYNE COXE. — Appointed by Edward Sheppard. Instituted, 1774.

30. NATHANIEL THORNBURY, LL.B.—Instituted, 1779. Appointed by Nathaniel Thornbury, gent., probably his father. Fosbroke says of him : " The present Rector, the Rev. Nath. Thornbury, is a gentleman well-known for his intimate acquaintance with most of the nations of Europe, which he repeatedly visited, as well as the greatest part of England. In Mineralogy, of which he has a most judiciously-selected

cabinet, he possesses great information, as well as in ancient and modern languages, and general knowledge of a liberal and elegant kind ; all which he enlivens by ability, vivacity and wit."

31. THOMAS BROOKE.—Instituted, 1816. The Gloucester Diocesan Records say he was appointed by Samuel Sheppard, but there was no Samuel Sheppard living at the time. The appointment may refer back to the settlement of the Living made by Samuel Sheppard, as stated above, but I think the Advowson had been parted with before 1816.

32. PHILIP BLISS, D.C.L.—Instituted, 1830. Appointed by J. F. Brooke and others. The Living had now passed into the hands of the Brooke Trustees.

This was an eminent Gloucestershire man, and deserves a short notice. Dr. Bliss was the only son of Rev. Philip Bliss, Rector of Dodington and Frampton Cotterell, in this County, and was born at Chipping Sodbury, Dec. 21, 1787. He was educated first at the Grammar School, Chipping Sodbury, and afterwards at the Merchant Taylors' School, where he remained till 1806, in which year he became a Scholar of St. John's College, Oxford, and in 1815 a Fellow of the same College and B.C.L., taking his D.C.L. degree in 1820. He was ordained in 1817 to a Curacy in Oxfordshire, and became Rector of Avening in 1830 as above. The Dictionary of National Biography says : " Parochial Preferment he never held." This, however, is a mistake, as he was undoubtedly appointed Rector of Avening, and his institution is mentioned in the Diocesan Records. In the Avening Registers there is only one entry of duty done by him, viz. : the baptism of a child on Aug. 8, 1830, probably when he came to take possession of the Living. I believe the explanation to be that he acted as a " warming-pan " for Thomas Richard Brooke, a minor, the heir of a family owning the advowson of Avening and a considerable estate at Horton, which is close to Chipping Sodbury, and, no doubt, he was well-known to Dr. Bliss. In 1836, Thomas Richard Brooke came of age and was ordained, and Dr. Bliss, making way for him, he became Rector of Avening.

Dr. Bliss was an eminent Bibliographer, his principal work being a new Edition of Anthony à Wood's "Athenæ Oxonienses," with additions and continuation. The original edition of the Athenæ Oxonienses, published in 1691-92, is

said, on the title page, to be "An exact history of all the
Writers and Bishops who have had their Education at the
University of Oxford from 1500 to 1690, to which are added
the Fasti or Annals for the said time." Dr. Bliss very much
enlarged and corrected this work, his Edition running to
4 vols. 4to., published between the years 1816-1820. His
interleaved copy of à Wood's original work is preserved in
the Bodleian Library. Doctor Bliss eventually died in 1857,
aged 70.

33. THOMAS RICHARD BROOKE.—Instituted, as stated
above, in 1836. On attaining his majority, he seems to have
presented himself to the Living, as, according to the Diocesan
Records, he was appointed by Thomas Richard Brooke.
Besides the property already mentioned, he had the accumula-
tions of a long minority, and was a wealthy man. He built
the new Rectory—a very fine house, in a beautiful situation,
but rather too large for the present income of the Living. He
remained at Avening till about 1854, when he retired and lived
abroad till 1857, keeping a Curate to do the services and attend
to the parish until he finally sold the Advowson. The building
of the New Rectory and general extravagance, I think, involved him in some difficulties.

34. FRANCIS DE PARAVICINI. — Instituted, 1857. Ap-
pointed by Thomas Richard Brooke, of whom he bought the
Advowson. The Living was twice sequestrated during this
Rector's incumbency.

35. EDGAR WILLIAM EDWARDS.—Instituted, 1897. The
present Rector.

CHAPTER XVII.

DR. GEORGE BULL, RECTOR OF AVENING AND BISHOP OF ST. DAVIDS

DR. George Bull was born at Wells, March 25th, 1634, and was ordained at the early age of 20. He showed his skill in dialectics and his readiness as a disputant whilst still an undergraduate at Oxford. His first benefice was St. George's, Bristol, and he seems at once to have fallen foul of the Quakers. As he was preaching one day a Quaker came into the Church and called out : " George, come down, thou art a false prophet and an hireling ; " whereupon the congregation fell upon the intruder with such fury that Bull was obliged to descend from his pulpit to save him from their violence.

The Restoration opened the way for Bull's preferment, and he was made Rector of St. Mary's, Siddington, and subsequently also of the adjoining parish of Siddington St. Peter's.

The following is an extract from Nelson's " Life of Dr. Bull " (2nd ed., pp. 80-81) :—

" The only Dissenters he had in this parish were Quakers who resisted all the endeavours he made to bring them into the Church, for they were as obstinate as they were ignorant, who by their impertinent and extravagant manner caused him no small uneasiness. And of this number was one who was a preacher among them, who would frequently accost Mr Bull ; and once more particularly, said he, ' George, as for human learning, I set no value upon it, but if thou wilt talk Scripture, have at thee.' Upon which Mr Bull, willing to correct his confidence, and to show him how unable he was to support his pretentions, answered him, ' Come on then, friend.' So opening the Bible which lay before them, he fell upon the Book of Proverbs. ' Seest thou, friend,' said he, ' Solomon saith in one place, "Answer a fool according to his folly," and in another place, "Answer not a fool according to his folly." How doest thou reconcile these two texts of Scripture ? ' ' Why,' said the preacher, ' Solomon don't say so.' To which Mr Bull replied, 'Aye, but he doth.' And turning to the places, soon convinced him ; upon which the Quaker, hereat being much out of countenance, said, ' Why, then Solomon was a fool,' which ended the controversy."

There were many passages-of-arms between Mr Bull and the Quakers, especially with one very well-known and excellent member of the Society of Friends, John Roberts, whose life, written by his son, was edited and reprinted by the late John Bellows. It is a most entertaining and interesting little book, and I recommend any one interested in Gloucestershire county history and quaint customs to read it.

John Roberts was a farmer living at Siddington, on a little estate of his own, and was, therefore, under the constant observation of Bull, the Rector of the parish, to whom he was extremely obnoxious and who frequently cast him into prison at Cirencester for non-payment of tithes. This probably occurred many times, as John consistently refused to pay. " For conscience sake," he said, " I can't pay a hireling priest what he demands of me ; therefore, he, like the false prophets of old, prepares war against me, because I cannot put into his mouth." On one of these occasions he was freed from prison by Lady Dunch, of Down Ampney, who frequently befriended him and often attended the meetings of the Friends, though I do not know whether she became a Quaker.

John Roberts had frequent interviews and conversation with William Nicholson, Bishop of Gloucester (1660-1671), who seems to have conceived a genuine liking and respect for him. At one of the interviews the following conversation occurred :—

JOHN ROBERTS : " I was bred up under a Common Prayer Priest, and a poor drunken old man he was ; sometimes he was so drunk he could not say his prayers ; though

I think he was a far better man then he who is priest there now."

BISHOP : " Who is your Minister now ? "

ROBERTS : " The present priest of the parish is George Bull."

BISHOP : " Do you say the drunken old man was better than Mr Bull ? I tell you that I account Mr Bull as sound, able and orthodox a divine as we have among us."

ROBERTS : " I am sorry for that, for if he be one of the best of you, I believe the Lord will not suffer you long ; for he is a proud, ambitious, ungodly man ; he hath often sued me at law and brought his servants to swear against me wrongfully. His servants themselves have confessed to my servants that I might have their ears (presumably in the pillory), for their master made them drunk and then told them they were set down in the list as witnesses against me ; and so they did, and brought treble damages. They also owned that they took tithes from my servant, thrashed them out and sold them for their master. They have also several times took my cattle out of my grounds to fairs and markets and sold them without giving me any account."

BISHOP : " I do assure you that I will inform Mr Bull of what you say."

ROBERTS : " And if thou pleasest to send for me to face him I shall make much more appear to his face than I'll say behind his back."

On another occasion the Bishop held a visitation at Tetbury, accompanied on the way by some of the leading gentry and clergy of the neighbourhood, including Parson Bull, and, passing John Roberts's house, they called there, and were hospitably entertained, the Bishop especially commending a new broached cask of beer. They all drank of it except Bull, who refused the cup offered him by Roberts, saying, " It is full of hops and heresy." To which Roberts replied, "As to hops I cannot say much, not being at the brewing of it, but as for heresy, I do assure thee, neighbour Bull, there is none in my beer. Here my Lord Bishop hath drunk of it and commends it ; he finds no heresy in the cup."

Bull was made a Prebendary of Gloucester by Lord Chancellor Finch, and installed October 9th, 1678, whilst still at Siddington. Subsequently, on July 10th, 1686, the degree of D.D. was conferred on him without the payment of the usual fees. The following account of his presentation to the living of Avening, and his subsequent ministry there, is taken from Nelson :—" It was in the year 1685 when Mr Bull was presented to the Rectory of Avening, in Gloucestershire, a large parish about 8 miles in compass, the income whereof is about £200 a year. The patron of it is Philip Sheppard, of Minching Hampton, Esquire, a very worthy gentleman eminent for his probity, sobriety and charity, and for his great usefulness in his county, for he not only administers justice with great impartiality, but endeavours to reconcile all quarrels and dissensions among his neighbours before they break into a flame, and before his neighbours lose their money and tempers in legal prosecutions, in which commonly both suffer.

" It happened that when this living became vacant Mr Sheppard and Mr Bull, with some other friends, were at Astrope-Wells, in Northamptonshire, drinking those mineral waters for the advantage of their health, and they were together with some other gentlemen when Mr Sheppard received the news of it (the vacancy of the living), upon which he acquainted the company that he had a very good living to dispose of, and reckoned up those qualifications he expected in the person upon whom he would bestow it ; which so exactly agreed to Mr Bull's character that every one present plainly perceived that Mr Sheppard designed to determine that preferment in Mr Bull's favour. But he had too much humility to make the application to himself, and therefore took not the least notice of it. Some time after Mr Bull withdrew with some of the company to walk in the garden, which opportunity Mr Sheppard took to declare that he had on purpose given those hints that Mr Bull might be encouraged to apply to him for it ; but finding his modesty was too great to take that step he was resolved to offer it to him who had more merit to deserve it than assurance to ask for it ; which accordingly he did as soon as Mr Bull returned into the room ; which he received with all those acknowledgments which were due for so good a living to so generous a patron.

George Bull D.D.
Late Lord Bishop of St Davids.
Ob: 17 Feb: 1709 Ætis 76.
Qui Magna non modo Locutus Est
sed et Vixit

GEORGE BULL, D.D.

"One of Dr. Bull's first cares on coming to Avening was the rebuilding of the parsonage house, part of which had been burnt down before he became Incumbent. This expense, the narrative continues, was very hard on a person who was never beforehand with the world ; but being necessary for the convenience of his family and the benefit of his successors, he cheerfully engaged in it."

" The people of the parish gave Mr Bull for some time great uneasiness and trouble ; there were many of them very loose and dissolute, and many more disaffected to the discipline and liturgy of the Church of England. This state and condition of the parish did not discourage Mr Bull from doing his duty, though it occasioned him many difficulties in the discharge of it, and he suffered many indignities and reproaches with admirable patience and Christian fortitude for not complying with those irregular practices which had long prevailed among them. But by steadfastness and resolution in performing his holy function, according to the Rubric, by his patient demeanour and prudent carriage, by his readiness to do them all offices of kindness, and particularly by his great charity to the poor, who in that place were very numerous, he did in the end remove all those prejudices which they had entertained against him, and reduced them to such a temper as rendered his labours effectual among them. In so much that they generally became constant in their attendance upon public worship and very decent in their behaviour at it, and, what was effected with the greatest difficulty, they brought their children to be baptised at Church ; for when all other arguments failed, the assurance he gave them that this was the practice of the Reformed Churches, persuaded them to comply without any further scruple. Indeed, by degrees the people, perceiving that he had no design upon them than their own good, of which they frequently experienced several instances, their aversion was changed into love and kindness ; and though at his first coming among them they expressed a great deal of animosity and disrespect to his person and family, yet many years before he left them they seemed highly sensible of their error and gave many signal proofs of their hearty goodwill towards him and them ; and when he was promoted from this parish to the Bishoprick of S. David no people could testify more concern and sorrow than the parishioners did upon this occasion for the loss of these advantages which they enjoyed by his living among them.   And I am credibly informed that to this day they never name him without expressions of gratitude and respect."

The above panegyric, extracted from Nelson, is in strange contrast to the account of Dr Bull given by John Roberts ; perhaps a little must be taken off both sides and allowance made for the times in which they lived.

Dr Bull was a very prolific writer on theological subjects ; he was a staunch upholder of the Established Church, and frequently had acrimonious controversies with other writers who did not agree with him in his ultra Protestantism.   He often preached on this subject, and very forcible sermons are mentioned as having been delivered at Bath, Gloucester, and at a visitation at Minchinhampton.   " Dr Bull was installed as Archdeacon of Llandaff, June 20th, 1686, bestowed upon him by Archbishop Sancroft, whose option it was, and principally in consideration of the great and eminent services he has done to the Church of God by his learned and judicious works."

He was consecrated Bishop of S. David's April 29th, 1705, and died at Brecon, February 17th, 1709, aged 75 years, and is buried there.   He had eleven children, all of whom except two died young and in his lifetime.   The only children who survived him were a son, who became Vicar of Tortworth and Prebendary of Gloucester, and a daughter.   The son married Rachel, daughter of Edward Stephens, of Cherington, and of Mary, daughter of Sir Matthew Hale.   Several of Dr Bull's children are buried at Avening.

On his tomb at Brecon is this inscription :—

<blockquote>
Here lieth the Right Reverend
Father in God Dr George Bull
Late Bishop of this Diocess
Who was excellently learned
Pious and charitable
And who departed this Life
February the 17th, 1709, Aged 75
</blockquote>

CHAPTER XVIII.

THE TOWN AND NEIGHBOURHOOD OF
MINCHINHAMPTON

MINCHINHAMPTON is one of the typical old Cotteswold towns left behind by the railways, and no longer, as formerly, the centre of the trade of the district, which has gradually left the old town and is now established in places more convenient and nearer to the all important railways, though a number of excellent old town houses, some of considerable architectural pretensions and mostly with beautiful old gardens attached, still remain to bear witness to its former importance. This prosperity was almost entirely due to the clothing industry, many of the principal houses within the town having been built by wealthy and retired clothiers, with whom it was a favourite place of residence. It may be proper to observe here that the old term " clothier " meant a " maker of cloth," and is so defined in Johnson's Dictionary, but it has now been usurped by the vendors of ready-made clothes. It is a designation of great antiquity and was well understood in old days. Shakespeare, for instance, makes Norfolk say in " King Henry VIII.," Act 1, Scene 2 :—

> " Upon these taxations
> The Clothiers all, not able to maintain
> The many to them 'longing, have put off
> The spinsters, carders, fullers, weavers."

Shakespeare has often been credited with a prophetic insight into future times, and he seems to have foreseen the exactions which had much to do with the downfall of the old clothiers, and the many new burdens placed by recent legislation on the industries of their successors, the cloth manufacturers of the present day.

There were originally three market houses in Minchinhampton, only one of which, built by Philip Sheppard about 1700, still remains. The site of the other two is doubtful, but from certain indications I think that one at least was built on the " Island" which is a block of buildings surrounded on all sides by streets of the town. Parsons in his MS. history mentions only two, but Rudder and Wantner say there were three. The latter gives the following account of them :—

> " The beauty of the towne consisteth in the four cross streets, which pointeth east, west, north and south, which is nobly adorned with three spacious market houses, one for white meat, one for corne, and the other for woll and yearn, the last of which was built by the Honoured and worthy gentleman, Philip Sheppard, Esquire, the present Lord of the Manor, which is a most noble pile of building, finished anno domini 1700. There is no market towne in this County (besides this) that hath three market houses belonging to it, whose chiefest dependence relyeth on their markets and faires, together with the clothing manufactorie which is the main support of all this part of ye countrie."

Notwithstanding the above, I believe that all three market houses were built as storing places for wool, where the clothiers from the valleys could meet the farmers from the hills, see the wool in bulk, and make their bargains with the owners. As less and less English wool was used, and more and more was imported from abroad, these market houses survived their usefulness, and two of them were accordingly pulled down and the materials sold. The market house which still stands is the very handsome building erected by Philip Sheppard and recently given to the town, on certain conditions, by Major Ricardo. When first I remember it the two floors which then existed were used as a school for boys and girls, and only ceased to be so used when the present schools were built in 1868.

There is a tradition that Mrs Siddons acted in the present market house. This may be well founded, as she lived and acted at Bath, between the years 1778 and 1782, occasionally going on tour. She was certainly at Stroud and also at

Cheltenham, and it is reasonable to suppose that she may have come to Minchinhampton at the invitation of one of the Sheppards, who were great patrons of the drama. She had so great a success at Cheltenham that Garrick sent his deputy to see her as "Calista" in Rowe's "Fair Penitent," and she was immediately engaged to appear at Drury Lane at a salary of £5 a week.

The Lammas, the beautiful residence of the Misses Baynes, has been through many vicissitudes, has passed through the hands of many owners, and has been called by many names. In the reign of Edward I. it appears to have been held by Peter de la Mere, who also held a lease from Malmesbury Abbey of the land on which St. Loe's School now stands, as mentioned in Chapter IX. It then went, according to Atkyns and Rudder, by the name of Delamere Manor, or Lamers, which latter name may have been a corruption and contraction of Delamere's. In the reign of Richard III. it passed to one George Nevile, and is called Lamers or Lambards, "near the spring of Minchinhampton." Finally under the name of the Lammas it passed to the Pinfolds, and from them, under the circumstances already narrated, to the Cockins. The late Mr C. R. Baynes bought the house and property from Mr Cockin's heir in 1876, and it remains in the possession of his representatives.

On the 13th December, 1790, a moiety of the estate "expectant on the decease of the survivor of the Miss Pinfolds," was offered by auction at the "Fleece Inn," Cirencester, but does not appear to have been sold. It is described as "that beautiful and delightful spot called the Lammas, consisting of a dwelling house, garden, fish ponds, pleasure grounds, etc." There was also a considerable amount of land and many cottages, but I do not think that the fish ponds can have been extensive, though perhaps sufficient to justify an auctioneer's advertisement, and probably consisted of the head of water at the bottom of the Well Hill which drove a grindstone for sharpening the shears used for clipping the face of the cloth after raising by the teazle. There is an ancient tithe barn at the back of the Lammas house, and on the site of the present house or very near it the ancient manor house is supposed to have stood. Bigland says: "The ancient manorial house inhabited by the Wyndesors is said to have been situate in the centre of the town and to have been very spacious, and to have had hanging gardens open to the south. The large mansion near the Church called the farm was occupied by the firmarius, or receiver, of Abbey rents." Philip Sheppard made it his residence, and altered and enlarged it considerably. The traces of the hanging gardens at the Lammas still exist.

Amongst other residents in the Parish of Minchinhampton, Edmund Clutterbuck, who lived at Hyde Court, was well-known and much respected. He was an Attorney-at-Law, and, as already mentioned, he acted as agent for two generations of Sheppards, eventually marrying Anne, daughter of Samuel (3rd), and dying Oct. 5, 1778, aged 71, during the time that Edward Sheppard held the family estates.

I have accidentally come into possession of a portion of his widow's accounts, which are most admirably and carefully kept, and contain her everyday expenditure from the death of her husband to her own death at the end of November, 1791, the last entry in her handwriting being written on Nov. 5th of that year.

Some of the entries are very quaint, and perhaps a few extracts may be given, as illustrating the expenditure of a family in a good position at this date.

One of the first entries is the amount spent on mourning for her husband, comprising both her own clothes and those of Molly, the daughter who lived with her, and also a moderate amount for the servants. The total expended on this mourning was £76 17s 9½d, but this does not include the funeral expenses, which were probably paid by the executors out of the estate.

Every month occurs the following :—
    " Pd. Mr Pearce for combing my curls 0. 0. 6."
And also frequent payments to the same for repairing or making " Roles."

This Pearce was one of a long line of barbers and hair-dressers at Minchinhampton, and the writer remembers to have been operated on by the last of the family.

The lady appears to have been fond of snuff, and to have consumed about 1 lb. every two months, which cost her 3s 6d. Snuff taking was very fashionable with ladies up to the beginning of the last century, as many of the pretty old snuff boxes bear witness ; cigarettes are now more in favour.

Mrs Clutterbuck was a most charitable lady, and her accounts are full of entries of gratuities to poor people. Amongst other subscriptions she gave £1 1s 0d to the Gloucester Infirmary, subsequently increased to £2 2s 0d. She also duly rewarded those who brought her presents from her brother of sucking pigs, hares, partridges, trout, etc., and on one occasion she received half a buck from Mr Coxe, of Kemble Park, who was related to her. Her daughter Molly received an allowance of £5 5s quarterly, and on one occasion £2 2s towards the expenses of a journey to Manchester, no doubt a great event. A grey mare was also bought for Molly, the price of which was £6 16s 6d. I hope the mare was a better one than its cost would seem to indicate. To her scapegrace nephew, Phil, she gave frequent " tips " of 5s, probably whenever he came to see her, and no doubt he knew where to get 5s when he wanted it.

The total expenditure, including the Household accounts which are, unfortunately, lost, ranged from £450 to about £600 a year. The following is a specimen of the accounts for the year 1781 :—

Total of Petty Cash Ledger £290 9 11
For cloths for myself   ..   63 10 0¼
For housekeeping from
Dec. ye 24th, 1780, to
Dec. ye 31st, 1781   ..   249 17 6¾

£603 17 6

The taxes, including poor rate, amounted to about £30, which does not seem excessive, except the item of £8 for a carriage. The window tax on 27 windows was £2 17s 0d. Another branch of the Clutterbuck family lived at Avening Lodge, now the residence of Mrs Calcutt, and held an estate there. Accordingly, we find an entry : " Pd. Mr Clutterbuck for Sunday School at Avening £1 1s 0d." One of the most frequent entries in these accounts is of money paid to Mrs Fowler, who seems to have been a celebrated woman in her day, judging from the following obituary notice which was published in a Bristol newspaper of Oct. 25, 1794.

" On Monday, at Minchinhampton, Mrs Mary Fowler, one of the people called Quakers, and perhaps the most opulent shopkeeper in the county of Gloucester. She was a capital woollen and linen draper, hosier, grocer and chandler. She supplied the whole neighbourhood with wines and spirits of every description, medicines, books and stationery, and was a most considerable dealer in oils and hops. In short not a single article that the particular manufactures of the neighbourhood demanded, but might be procured in abundant quantities at her extensive warerooms." The writer concludes with an eulogium on her personal virtues.[1]

Amongst the principal residences in the Parish of Minchinhampton are Gatcomb, already mentioned, the property of Major (now Lt.-Col.) Ricardo, and Longfords, the home of the writer. The latter has externally no special architectural features, though placed in a beautiful situation. The ancient home of the family, and before them of the Pinfolds, was in a courtyard adjoining the mill, all trace of which, except the great kitchen chimney corner, has disappeared. There are many other good houses in the neighbourhood, and round the sides of Hampton Common, the beauty of the scenery and the healthiness of the situation making it a favourite place of residence.

In Avening the principal house is Avening Court, the ancient Manor House, but this has been so extensively altered that but little of the old building remains. It is now the property of Mr Martin Viner Pollock, whose mother inherited it as last in the entail created by her great grandfather, William Playne, senr., her father, Capt. F. C. Playne of the Rifle Brigade, having died in 1863. There are other good houses in Avening, especially the new Rectory already mentioned as having been built by the Rev. T. R. Brooke.

St. Loe's School

The name of this school has given rise to much controversy and many suggestions have been made as to its origin. Locally it used to be called " Sinkley," and from this in later times was evolved " St. Chloe." Another suggestion is " Saintlieu," or Holy Place, on account of its having been held by Malmesbury Abbey; and the Charity Commissioners have fixed on St. Loe, it being described in the deed of the original foundation as " Saintloe, *alias* Seinckley." But Mr St. Clair

Baddeley, in his recently published and most valuable hand-book on " Gloucestershire Place Names," traces the name back to Saxon times, where, in a charter of Ethelbald, King of the Mercians (A.D. 716, 743) it appears as *Sengedleag*.

The School was founded by Nathaniel Cambridge, a Ham-burgh merchant, who left a sum of £1,000 by will to be invested in land by 11 named trustees, all of whom with one exception (William Kingscote, of Kingscote) are described as Clothiers. The foundation deed states that the school is for the education of boys born, or to be born, in the parish of Woodchester, or that part of the parish of Minchinhampton which is in the tything of Rodborough. The trustees bought the house and small estate, which is still the property of the foundation, the purchase being completed on June 1, 1699. By Cambridge's bequest, the master of the school, after paying all taxes and repairs, took the balance as his salary, an arrangement which did not tend to the upkeep of the premises in the best possible repair. Nevertheless the school has frequently had very good masters, and at one time it held a high position in the neigh-bourhood as an educational institution. The school house is a very interesting old building, with immensely thick walls, and a courtyard in the centre. In the great schoolroom there was a circular staircase built in the thickness of the wall, which gave access to an upper floor, now done away with. It stands in a very attractive situation overlooking the Wood-chester valley, and is now occupied as a private dwelling house. The school has been twice re-organised by the Charity Com-missioners, and the income of the foundation is now devoted to scholarships and apprenticeships.

In a garden at Nailsworth, belonging to Miss Tabram, and within the ancient Parish of Avening, are the remains of a Chapel, probably of 14th century work. It was formerly used as a stable and afterwards as an office, but it is now closed and well taken care of. The Chapel has consequently been much maltreated in former times, but sufficient remains of the ancient building to enable its original plan to be easily traced. The main walls and the lower part of the east window are still there, and also a piscina and an ancient doorway. The present east window was brought from some other build-ing, and does not belong to the original structure. Close to the Chapel is a very old house, supposed to have been the

Priest's lodging. There was a circular staircase in this house, removed about 40 years ago. Rudder mentions this Chapel and says there was another at Aston also within the ancient Parish of Avening, but its situation cannot now be identified.

The only record of a Priest at Nailsworth occurs as already mentioned in Walker's " Sufferings of the Clergy," where one Thomas Worden is said to have come from Chipping Norton and to have been an intruder.

CHAPTER XIX.

MINCHINHAMPTON COMMON

THIS celebrated and beautiful expanse of downland was, until quite recent years, but little known and rarely visited by strangers. The extent of common land was formerly said to have been 1,000 acres, and, considering that in the case of enclosures sanctioned by the Common Committee of the Court Leet, a double quantity of land to that taken in was always thrown out elsewhere, and considering also the recent purchase by the Golf Club of the great park at Minchinhampton extending to 30 acres, the present area cannot be much, if any, less than it formerly was. By the last named addition the Common is brought up close to the town, with great advantage to the owners of adjacent building land. The Great Park was part of the pleasure grounds of the old Sheppard House, the entrance gates of which are still to be seen, and it was also the site of the Great Trees mentioned in Chap. VII.

The rights of the Commoners have always been jealously safeguarded, and encroachments rigorously suppressed. Nothing arouses greater local feeling than any attempt, real or supposed, to encroach on the rights of the Commoners, and it is owing to this strong feeling that, whilst other Commons have been enclosed, notably towards the close of the 18th century, this noble expanse of pasture has been preserved for the benefit of the parishioners of Minchinhampton and for the enjoyment of all who visit it.

There were formerly many presentments to the Court Leet at its annual meetings alleging that certain persons had encroached or otherwise damaged the Common, and in 1832 especially the following notice was issued to supposed delinquents : " In consequence of the numerous encroachments that have been made upon Minchinhampton Common, a meeting of the inhabitants was called, and it was then resolved that a Committee should be appointed for the purpose of resisting them. From the information received it appears that a part of the land in your occupation belongs to Minchinhampton Common, and I am therefore directed by the Committee to inform you that they will sit at the vestry room on April 17th, between the hours of 10 and 3, and, unless they hear further from you, they intend to claim it, and will take measures to restore it to the Common." This notice is signed by Fenning Parke, but I am unable to say what effect it had. Many regulations have from time to time been made, and, finally, by a deed dated April 7th, 1913, Major Ricardo, Lord of the Manor of Minchinhampton, has relinquished all his Manorial rights over the Common, and transferred them to the " National Trust for Places of Historic Interest or Natural Beauty." This transfer has so recently come into effect that it is too early to say whether or not it is to the advantage of the town and neighbourhood. Perhaps it will make but little difference, if the new owners are reasonable, and the only present effect of the transfer has been that the quarrying of stone has been stopped, no doubt to the advantage of the pasture, but throwing many out of employment, and the far-famed and beautiful building stone will no longer be available.

In the centre of the Common stands an ancient enclosure called the " Old Lodge," consisting of an inn, stables and garden, and a large and ancient bowling green. There is a tradition that Charles I. stopped and dined at the " Old Lodge," and that he or some of his suite played a game of bowls on the green. If there is any truth in this tradition, the incident must have occurred in the flying visit which Charles made to Oxford from Matson House, during the siege of Gloucester, as that is the only time he could have passed over Minchinhampton Common. The first mention I have been able to find of the " Old Lodge " is in a deed of conveyance from Lord Windsor to Samuel Sheppard and his son Philip, dated May 28th, 1656. The deed recites that,

> " Thomas Windesor, Lord Windesor, for, and in consideration of the sum of Two Thousand Five Hundred and Thirty Pounds of lawful money of England, to the

said Thomas Windesor Lord Windesor in hand, at and before ensealeing and delivery of these presents by the said Samuel Sheppard, truly paid . . . . . . by these presents hath granted, bargayned, sold, aliened, released and confirmed, and by these presents att and by the nomynation and appointment of the said Samuel Sheppard, doth fully and absolutely grante, bargayne, sell, alien, release, and confirm unto the said Philip Sheppard in his actual possession . . . . . . all that great Wood or Woodground, lying and being in Avening in the county of Gloucester, commonly knowne or called by the name of Hazelwood conteyneing by estimation three hundred acres . . . . . and all those several Wood Coppices and Wood Grounds, commonly called Gattcombe, Amberley Green, Amberley Coppice, *and the Lodge thereon built* . . . . . all lying and being within the townes, parishes, feilds and Terretories of Minchinhampton and Avening aforesaid."

The deed from which these extracts are taken is of considerable length and is signed by Thomas Windesor, and has a fine seal with the Windsor Arms. By this signature it seems that the barony was not called out during the Commonwealth. The deed is witnessed by " Will Sheppard, Robert Abbot and Richard Lloyd," and below is the note : "Acknowledged 30th May, 1656, before me—Will Sheppard."

By the above we may conclude that, though purchased by Samuel, it passed at once into the possession of his son and heir, Philip, possibly to avoid some taxations.

This also seems to confirm the tradition that a considerable amount of enclosed land once adjoined the Old Lodge, and that a rabbit warren also existed there. But all traces of enclosures have now disappeared and, if they did exist, I have no information as to when and under what circumstances they became Common land.

On many parts of Minchinhampton Common, and extending close into the town, and even beyond, are the well-known earthworks. Opinions differ greatly as to the period to which they belong and for what purpose they were constructed. They vary considerably in depth and width, and there seems to be no method in their plan. Some of the trenches are shallow, and, unless fenced with palisades, would afford no protection from enemies. They may have been constructed by the pit dwellers for the protection of themselves and their animals, if they possessed any, but the larger ones were probably constructed at a much later period and were perhaps successively used by Romans, Saxons and Danes. Minchinhampton Common, with its steep escarpments, would be easily defensible, and would probably not be neglected in warlike times, but whatever their history, the earthworks are remarkable and interesting features in the landscape. The Common has always been a favourite place for sports of various kinds. Formerly a cricket ground was kept mown and rolled near the Old Lodge, and football is frequently played there. There used to be race meetings also, the last of which I have a record taking place in 1827. Bull baiting, I regret to say, was a frequent occurrence the last occasion being in 1817, when a bull was baited at the Cross in the town. But the principal event in more recent times, and one which has brought the Common into greater prominence, was the establishment of the Golf Club in 1889. Since then houses have sprung up and numerous lodgings have been furnished for letting. The healthiness of the locality and the beauty of the scenery make it a favourite resort in summer holidays. Many people with business in Gloucester and elsewhere in the Vale live here and find it a delightful change to pure hill air. Golf was perhaps not very popular with some of the Commoners at first, but it is now recognized that it does no damage and that its establishment has brought great prosperity to the district.

There is on Minchinhampton Common an old British tumulus, which has been so maltreated that it is difficult to trace its original shape, but it has in recent times a remarkable history, for here the celebrated divine George Whitefield preached to enormous congregations, and from this circumstance it has been known as " Whitefield's Tump," and we must now give an account of some important events which happened in connection with Whitefield's congregation at Minchinhampton.

GEORGE WHITEFIELD

The celebrated preacher and divine George Whitefield was a frequent vistor to Minchinhampton, often preaching there and in the neighbourhood, and the following facts

THE REV.ᴰ GEORGE WHITEFIELD. A·M.

Chaplain to the Countess of Huntingdon.

THE REV. GEORGE WHITEFIELD

taken from his diaries and letters will be of interest to Minchinhampton parishioners.

George Whitefield was born at Gloucester, December 16th, 1714, the last year of the reign of Queen Anne. He was the youngest son of his father, who kept the Bell Inn at Gloucester, and who died when George was only two years old. He was educated at the College, and Crypt Grammar Schools, and between the years of 12 and 15 he made great progress in the Latin classics, early displaying that eloquence which so distinguished him in after life. At the age of 18 he went to Oxford, where he was " exposed to the society of the wicked." Fortunately he came under the influence of Charles Wesley, and he joined a society of Methodists. Having taken his degree, he was ordained by Bishop Benson, of Gloucester, and after staying some time in England, often preaching to enormous concourses of people, he paid his first visit to America in 1737, returning in the following year. In all he paid three visits to America, and ultimately died at Newbury Port, U.S.A., aged 56. In March, 1743, he writes in his diary : " Then I rode to Stroud and preached to about 12,000 people in Mrs. G.'s field, and about 6 in the evening to a like number on Hampton Common." No doubt he spoke from " Whitefield's Tump." The diary proceeds : "After this, went to Hampton and held a general love feast and went to bed about mid-night very cheerful and happy." In a letter written March 12, 1744, he says : " Wiltshire has been very remarkable for mobbing and abusing the Methodists, and for about 10 months past it has also prevailed very much in Gloucestershire, especially at Hampton, where Mr Adams has a house and has been much blessed to many people. About the beginning of July last they assembled in great numbers with a low bell and horn, broke the windows and mobbed the people to such a degree that many expected to be murdered and hid themselves in holes and corners. Once when I was there they continued from four till mid-night rioting, giving loud huzzas, casting dirt upon the hearers and declaring that none should preach there on pain of being put into a skin pit and afterwards into a brook. On the 10th July they came to the number of near 300, forced into Mr Adams' house and demanded him down the stairs whereon he was preaching, took him out of the house, threw him into

¹ Notes and Queries, Ser. II, vii., 384-5.

a skin pit full of noisome things and stagnated water. One of our friends named Williams asked them " if they were not ashamed to use an innocent man so ? " They threw him into the same pit and dragged him along the kennel. Mr Adams quietly returned and betook himself to prayer, exhorting the people to rejoice in suffering for the sake of the Gospel. In about half an hour they returned and led him away to a place called Bourne Brook and threw him in. A bystander rescued him but they threw him in again. After this there was no more preaching for some time, the people fearing to assemble on account of the violence of the mob." Thereupon an information was laid in the King's Bench against five of the rioters, and the trial was held at Gloucester Assizes. Of course, the other side gave a different account of the occurrences, but the verdict was in favour of the Methodists. I do not find that any penalty was inflicted, and Whitefield says that they were only anxious to let them see what they could do, and then forgive them. No doubt the Methodists were maltreated in this case, as in others, but it must be remembered that we have the evidence of one side only and the accusations were stoutly denied by the defendants. Mr Adams, who at that time was at Minchinhampton, lived afterwards at Rodborough, where he built and endowed the Tabernacle, " for the sole use and benefit of a certain society of people who profess to be of the Calvinistic principles pursued and upheld by the late Rev. George Whitefield."

However much we may regret these persecutions of the Methodists, we must remember that the Clergy of the Established Church also suffered greatly during the Civil War and Commonwealth, and none more grievously than the Rev. Henry Fowler, the Rector of the same Parish in which the above events occurred. We may be thankful that we live in better and more enlightened times, and that persecutions in the name of Religion have long ceased to exist.

CHAPTER XX.

THE TRADES OF THE DISTRICT.

THE CLOTHING TRADE.

IN writing the history of the trades of the district, nothing is more remarkable than the number of those engaged in the making of woollen cloth, or in the various processes through which a piece of cloth passes from the time the wool leaves the sheep's back until the finished article is completed. The Monuments in the churches and churchyards bear witness to the number of those connected with the trade ; and, besides the Masters, there was a multitude of humbler workers, such as the weavers, spinners and others, so that it appears as though the whole population, except the Landowners and those engaged in the actual cultivation of the soil, were dependent on the clothing industry for their livelihood. And even to the farmers the trade was of great advantage, as the yearly clip of wool materially added to the value of their sheep.

I propose to trace the changes which have occurred, from early times, in the fabric itself, in the wool from which it is made, and in the methods by which it was manufactured.

[1] " *Wool* is a modified form of hair distinguished by its soft and wavy or curly structure, and, as seen under the microscope, by its highly imbricated or serrated surface." It is important to remember this distinguishing feature of wool, as compared with hair, in order to understand subsequent processes of manufacture.

The arts of spinning and weaving are of great antiquity. They were known to the Egyptians in very ancient times,

[1] Encyclop. Britt. Article Wool.

and Pliny mentions the various kinds of wool and the fabrics made in his day ; and among the arts which Britain owes to the Romans, not the least important is the spinning and weaving of wool.   The sheep, however, was a domestic animal in Britain long before the Roman occupation, and it is probable that some use was made by our earlier ancestors of sheep skins and wool ; and the matting of the wool on the sheep's back may even have suggested the felting process.   But the Romans, early in their occupation, established wool factories, notably at Winchester, whence their legions were supplied with clothing.   The Britons were not slow to see the value of the manufacture, and, as mentioned by Tacitus, soon began to use the new material, and before long to make it for themselves.

There are many allusions to the woollen manufacture in Britain in ancient times, but the native industry could not rival the products of the Continent, though the wool spun from the English fleece was highly prized abroad, and is said to have been " spun so fine that it is in a manner comparable to a spider's thread."

The wool grown on our Cotteswold Hills was held in high reputation in ancient times, and we read that " the inhabitants are so wise, and they make such improvements of their wool, that their sheep may be said to bear golden fleeces to them." Towards the end of the fourteenth century and the begin- ning of the fifteenth, the woolstaplers of the Cotteswolds rose to great wealth and prosperity, and many of our noblest churches, especially at Chipping Campden and Fairford, bear witness to their munificence.   William Grevel, described on his tombstone as " *Flos Mercatorum lanarum totius Angliæ*," was a most generous benefactor to Chipping Campden Church and Town.   John Tame, also a wealthy woolstapler, re-built Fairford Church to receive the world-famous glass with which he adorned it ; and there are many more instances, as at Northleach, Cirencester, and other places, of generous bene- factions by these princely merchants.

Some attempts were made for the improvement of manu- factures by William the Conqueror, who imported and pro- tected Flemish weavers, and Henry II. also established a Cloth Fair in the churchyard of St. Bartholomew the Great. It was not, however, till the reign of Edward III. that special efforts were made to encourage woollen industries. Fuller, in his Church History, says :—

> " King Edward III., seeing the great gains of the Netherlanders, resolved to introduce the clothing art to our countrymen," of whom he disrespectfully adds : " They knew no more what to do with their wool than the sheep that wears it, as to any artificial or curious drapery, their best cloth then being no better than friezes, such their coarseness for want of skill in the making."

Edward imported weavers, dyers and fullers from Flanders, and he himself, further to encourage the native trade, wore British cloth, as an example to his subjects, let us hope of better quality than that described by Fuller. He also prohibited, on pain of life or limb (having the right hand struck off), the exportation of British wool, which had a great reputation on the Continent, exceeded only by that of Spain. A wiser policy prevailed in the reign of Elizabeth, when the free exportation of wool was allowed, to the great advantage of the English sheep owners, and with the result that, during this reign, the manufacture of cloth made more rapid progress than at any previous time. No doubt it was also greatly stimulated by the many refugees, who fled to England to avoid the Spanish persecutions in the Netherlands, bringing their arts with them. This short-sighted policy of prohibiting the export of wool was again enacted on the Restoration in 1660, giving rise to a great deal of wool running and smuggling, and the prohibition was not finally removed till 1825.

In order to induce the clothworkers of the Netherlands to settle in England, emissaries were sent over, who, in the language of Fuller, represented to the journeymen their hard condition,

> " used rather like heathen than Christians, yea, rather like horses than men ; early up and late in bed, and all day hard work and harder fare (a few herrings and mouldy cheese). But oh ! how happy should they be if they would only come over into England, bringing their mystery with them. Here they should feed on fat beef and mutton, till nothing but their fulness should stint their stomachs."

As an additional inducement, the prospect of marrying English wives was held out to them, " and such the English beauties that the most curious foreigners cannot but commend them." These arguments prevailed with many, as, " persuaded with the promises, many Dutch servants leave their masters and make over to England," and fortunately the promises seem to have proved true, as we read : " Happy the yeoman's house into which one of these Dutchmen did enter, bringing industry and wealth along with them ; such as came in strangers within doors soon went out bridegrooms and returned sons-in-law, having married the daughters of their land-lords who first entertained them ; and those yeomen in whose houses they harboured soon became gentlemen and gained great estates to themselves."

The above is confirmed by the history of the family to which the present writer belongs. Originally refugees or immigrants from the Netherlands, they settled in Kent about the middle of the sixteenth century, and appear in the next generation to have been allied to some of the leading gentry of the County. The name was variously spelt as " de la Plaigne and de la Plane ; " the prefix seems to have dis-appeared in the second generation, as we find it as " Plane, Plaine, and Playne." Wyatt Plaine, who held lands in East Peckham and Hadlow, as is proved by a Deed in my possession, dated 1590, died at East Peckham in 1598, and is buried there. (In connection with Wyatt Plaine it is a curious coincidence that the writer is a direct descendant, through the Twisdens, of Sir Thomas Wyatt, the poet and courtier of Henry VIII., whose son was beheaded in 1554 for attacking and nearly capturing the Tower of London at the head of " The Men of Kent." Allington Castle, the residence of the Wyatts, now in ruins, is not far distant from East Peckham, and no doubt there was a connection between the families.)

In the next and subsequent generation the name became Playne, and Thomas Playne, son of Wyatt, appears to have married one of the Idens, as his son and grandson were both named Iden Playne, the Idens being a well-known and ancient Kentish family. About the year 1650 the Playnes disappear in Kent and re-appear again in Gloucestershire and Hereford-shire, and probably this was the time when they established themselves in this Valley ; but there was a further immigration in 1622, this entry appearing in the Dover Register : " Came from France by reason of the late troubles, Jean de la Plaigne, linen weaver." Besides the persecutions, he was probably attracted by the prosperity of his namesakes and relatives. Great Chart, in Kent, where some of the family appear in the Registers, was almost the centre of the industry in the Weald of Kent, and Hasted, in his History of Kent, says of the clothiers there : " They are a body so numerous and united that at County Elections whoever has their votes and interest is almost certain of being elected."

In the reign of Edward I. the office of "Aulnager " was instituted ; the name is derived from the French " aulne," an ell. The duties of this official were to " measure the cloth and mark the same, by which a man may know how much the cloth containeth. His fee of the seller shall be for every cloth a halfpenny, for every half-cloth a farthing, nothing for less than half a cloth, nor for anything but for cloths exposed for sale." The duty of the Aulnager does not seem always to have been carried out with much care, as in the reign of Richard II. it was enacted " Forasmuch as divers plain cloths wrought in the counties of Somerset, Dorset, Bristol and Gloucester be tacked and folded together and set to sale, of which cloths a great part be broken, ' broused,' and not agreeing in colour nor in no manner to the part of the same cloth shown outwards, but falsely wrought with divers wools, to the great deceit, loss and damage to the people, insomuch that the Merchants that buy the same and carry them out of the realm to sell to strangers, be many times in danger to be slain, and sometimes imprisoned and put to fine and ransom, therefore it is ordained that no plain cloth tacked and folded shall be set to sale within the said counties."

The above Act does not say much for the honesty of some of our clothier forefathers, and there is another in the reign of Henry VI. which is equally discreditable to the weavers : " Because the weavers in this realm be accustomed when they have wrought a cloth near to the end, to cut away for their private profit the thread that is unwoven and call the same ' thrums ' which they do sell to such persons as carry them into Flanders and under colour of such 'thrums' divers persons do carry great quantities of woollen yarn, to the hindrance of the King's customs, all such export is forbidden."

During the disorders and persecutions of the Civil War, and, in fact, during the whole of the long drawn-out conflict between the King and the Parliament, the cloth trade declined apace. Many clothiers were ruined, and many more left the country to avoid the persecutions and exactions to which they were subjected. So deplorable was the state to which the woollen trade had sunk, that in the reign of Charles II. a strange law was passed for its benefit. It was enacted that all corpses must be buried in woollen shrouds or in grave clothes of the same material, without admixture of any other, and it was gravely set out that this would also benefit the papermakers by freeing a great quantity of linen hitherto used in burial, linen being the material from which the best paper was then made. The penalty for burying a corpse in any material not entirely made of sheep's wool, "in any shift, sheet or shroud made or mingled with flax, hemp, silk, hair, gold or silver" was £5, and the clergyman officiating at the burial was also required to demand a certificate, "duly sworn and sealed before a Justice of the Peace," declaring that the body was so buried, and he was then also required to make entry in the Register that all these formalities had been complied with. This vexatious interference with people in their saddest moments was greatly resented, and many preferred to pay the fine rather than comply with the law. Some openly disregarded it, and Mr Blunt, in his "Dursley and its Neighbourhood," quotes the following caustic lines by Pope (Moral Essays, Ep. I. iii.) on the burial in 1731 of the celebrated actress, Ann Oldfield, "in a Brussels lace head dress, a Holland shift with tucks, and double ruffles of the same, and a pair of new kid gloves."

"Odious! in Wollen! 'twould a Saint provoke,"
    Were the last words that poor Narcissa spoke,
"No, let a charming chintz and Brussels lace
    Wrap my cold limbs and shade my lifeless face,
    One would not sure be frightful when one's dead,
    And—Betty—give this cheek a little red."

This Act was not repealed till 1814, and, though no longer compulsory, the custom still lingers, especially in the North of England.

The manufacturers of the eighteenth century were in a very small way of business compared with modern times, and some had not even a mill in which to make their cloth. They would buy a few bales of wool, say at Minchinhampton, or some other wool market, and all subsequent processes were carried out by the spinners and weavers in the cottages, or on commission at one of the mills. In Bigland is a woodcut showing a man riding past Avening Church, on one horse laden with wool, and driving another similarly laden in front of him.

Strikes.

So far, the woollen trade in Gloucestershire has been little interfered with by strikes, even when the business was more profitable than it is at present, and when all the Mills, now devoted to other trades, were working full swing at the fine West of England broadcloth and similar fabrics. The greatest strike which has occurred in this neighbourhood was the great strike of the hand loom weavers in 1825, for an increase of wages and for equalising prices for the work. It lasted for three months, and about 5,000 weavers and many thousands of workers in subsidiary trades were thrown out of employment. It was enforced by the leaders of the movement on their fellows by strong parties visiting the weavers in their homes and demanding the surrender of their shuttles, thus rendering them perforce idle. Towards the end of the time a very rancorous spirit prevailed towards those who showed signs of weakening, and in many cases they proceeded to violence (peaceful picketing !) The usual procedure was to take the beam out of the offender's loom, and mounting the poor weaver astride of it, to take him to the nearest canal or pond and tumble him into it. So many suffered in this way at Chalford, and so much violence prevailed, that the Magistrates were at length compelled to read the Riot Act and send for a troop of Horse to keep order, who carried out their duty very effectually. An amusing story is told of one of these Troopers. They were engaged in breaking up groups of rioters in Stroud, some of whom climbed into a wagon standing near, and from that safety, as they imagined, ventured to jeer and boo at the soldiers. The latter were not inclined to be made fools of in this way, and one of the number jumped his horse into the wagon and scattered the occupants, who fled from the wagon a great deal quicker than they had climbed into it.

The strike soon after came to an end, having occasioned great loss both to employers and employed and great distress among many innocent victims, who would gladly have continued to work had they been allowed. With the exception of this strike, there have been very few disputes in the woollen trade in this district between masters and workmen, and long may the good feeling which now exists continue with us, as disputes and strikes are beneficial neither to the one nor to the other.

The strike of the weavers was followed by a severe monetary crisis, which compelled more than half the bankers in the County to put up their shutters, and caused widespread distress. It was during this panic that William Playne, Senior, saved the Tetbury Bank under very similar circumstances to those detailed by Mrs Craik in " John Halifax, Gentleman." Mr Playne was at the time in London, and, anticipating that his Bankers at Tetbury would be hard pressed, he collected every sovereign he could by any means scrape together, took a chaise and four horses and galloped to Tetbury, where he arrived to find the Bank surrounded by a large crowd clamouring for their money and the cash drawer nearly empty. Very likely the amount which Mr Playne had been able to collect on so short a notice was not large, but seeing his well-known stalwart figure, followed by a servant carrying bags of gold, the depositors raised a hearty cheer, the run was stopped and the Bank was saved.

But, nevertheless, the acute monetary crisis brought great commercial depression in its train, with the inevitable consequence of a general reduction of wages. A different system also came into vogue which threw many of the old weavers out of employment. Up to this time cloth was not woven at the mills but by the master weavers, who employed journeymen to work for them, no doubt at very low wages, or else it was woven in the cottages by men working on their own account ; and it was a common sight to see outside the mills a number of horses or donkeys tethered at the entrance, either bringing back woven cloth or taking home chains and bobbins to weave others. This system had always been troublesome, and the ill-advised Beerhouse Act of 1830 had very much increased drunkenness amongst the weavers, never a very sober class, with the inevitable consequence of bad work. The larger manufacturers, therefore, now began to build loom sheds, in which all the hand-loom weavers required could be accommodated on the premises, and the work done under the immediate supervision of the employer. This again threw many of the less competent workmen out of employment, and the disaster was completed by the general adoption of the Power Loom in 1836. A few of the hand-loom weavers continued to work in the cottages, and I remember to have heard the shuttles going at the Box and elsewhere, but the race gradually died out or left the country, and though piteous appeals for work were frequently made at the mills, it was impossible for the manufacturers, under the stress of competition, to go back to the old and more expensive system. It was possible to employ a few hand-loom weavers on the more delicate material, but as the Power Loom became more perfect this also ceased.

So great was the distress and consequent discontent in 1838, that a Royal Commission was appointed to enquire into the state of things prevailing in the Clothing Trades. The Commissioner for this district was Mr W. A. Miles, who made a most exhaustive enquiry into the general condition of things, taking the evidence of all the leading manufacturers and also of some of the workpeople. The enquiry embraced many subjects, such as the condition of the weavers and their wages, the beer shops, the infamous Truck System, and there are many interesting chapters on Education, Benefit Clubs, Allotments, Emigration, etc. This Blue Book is a most valuable and interesting record and reflects great credit on the writer. I wish it were possible to give an analysis of Mr Miles's Report, but the subject is too large to include in this sketch.

Sir William Marling, in his interesting paper on the Woollen Trade, read at the opening of the winter session of the Stroud Textile School, in 1908, says :—

" On the whole, Mr Miles's recital is a sad one, and in striking contrast to the happier conditions prevailing in the Stroud valley to-day. Various remedies were devised to cope with this distress ; amongst others, the cultivation of allotment gardens and the encouragement of migration to other districts where labour was more in demand, while not a few benevolent residents in the district exerted themselves in assisting emigration. Some parishes, such as Uley and Bisley, borrowed money for this purpose, and Mr Miles gives a statement of the cost of emigrating 68 persons from Bisley Parish, who sailed on Aug. 31, 1837, from Bristol. The total cost of these 68 persons was £191 3s 1d, the whole of which sum was defrayed by public subscription or by borrowing on the security of the rates."

All the evidence produced before Mr Miles went to show that strikes only made the situation of the hand-loom weavers worse, while at the same time many Manufacturers were ruined, thereby increasing the unemployment, and tending to the lowering of wages, the supply of hand-loom weavers being far in excess of the demand.

Mr Miles gives a table of wages in 1839, which were much lower than at the present day, yet far in excess of those earned by the hand-loom weavers :—

Masons earned 15s to 17s a week, Blacksmiths, Carpenters and Plasterers 15s, and Labourers 9s, with cottage and garden and extra at Harvest.

In the Cloth trade the following were the weekly wages paid :—

Wool Sorters	30s.
Wool Scourers	14s
Wool Pickers (Women)	6s
Wool Feeders (Children)	3s
Mule Spinners (men)	20s
Warpers (Women)	7s
Millmen	20s
Burlers (Women)	6s
Shearmen	13s
Brushers	14s
Drawers and Markers (Women)	9s
Spinners (Women)	6s

The week always meant 60 working hours, and sometimes more.

Sir William Marling gives a picture of one of these hand-loom weavers, which I can confirm from my own recollection of many a one I have seen in bygone days.

"A middle-aged or elderly man, rather sad faced (at least, looking as though he had never been young), and often quaintly dressed—sometimes in a blue frock-coat with copper buttons, once gilt, or in a swallow-tailed one, once black, but now grown green with age (presumably some gentleman's left-off garment)."

Sir William might have added his battered old beaver top hat, which the poor weaver almost universally wore when coming to the mills in his best clothes, a truly pathetic figure, and I can to this day remember the keen disappointment on his face when told that there was no yarn for him to take home with him.

In the next chapter I propose to give an account of the gradual evolution of the methods of cloth making, from the time when nearly all the processes through which the cloth passed were carried out by manual labour, without motive power of any kind, up to the present time when machinery has taken the place of hand labour, and has reached such a pitch of perfection that no further great improvement can be looked forward to, though, no doubt, there are some minor inventions and economies still to come.

This gradual development will best be illustrated by tracing the history of one firm through all these stages, and for this purpose I cannot do better than give an account of a portion of the story of the firm to which I belong, and trace the changes and vicissitudes through which it has passed from the later years of the 18th century to the present time.

CHAPTER XXI.

THE TRADES OF THE DISTRICT

THE CLOTHING TRADE (*continued*)

I HAVE but few records of the firm of William Playne & Co. previous to the year 1788, many valuable old books and papers having been destroyed in a disastrous fire which occurred in 1836, by which the offices and the greater part of the old dwelling-house at Longfords were burnt out.

Longfords Mills, together with a small estate, were bought by Thomas Playne, great-grandfather of the writer, in 1759. The business had been carried on for many generations at Frogmarsh, in the parish of Woodchester, where part of the very Flemish-looking mill-buildings are still to be seen. The dwelling-house of the family was situated not far off, at Somerwells, two gables of the old house being still visible, incorporated with what is now the Franciscan Convent, built within recent years. Thomas Playne sold all he possessed in the parish of Woodchester on purchasing Longfords, and died in 1788, leaving a large family, of whom William Playne was the eldest but one. He was a boy of only 16 at the time of his father's death, and had recently left St. Loe's school, where he was educated. The affairs of Thomas Playne were in rather a state of confusion at the time of his death, but fortunately he left behind him a very capable son, and a widow, whose portrait by Rippingille is that of a very able and energetic woman, as she proved herself to be in the bringing up of her large family of eleven children. The firm was reconstituted under the name of " Martha Playne & Son," and before many years had passed all liabilities had been discharged and the business placed on a solid foundation. In the year 1797 Martha Playne retired, and the firm became William Playne & Co. In 1801 another change occurred

MARTHA PLAYNE

owing to Peter Playne, the third son of Martha Playne, coming into the firm, which, until 1828, became William & Peter Playne.

I do not know what amount of English wool was used at Longfords before the year 1790, but from that time onwards the cloth was made of Spanish wool, and it is probable that for many years English wool had only been used in small quantities for the lists (selvage) and for forels and tags or head and tail ends of the finer cloth. The average price of Spanish wool in 1790 would be about 3s to 3s 6d per lb.—not a high price for the grower when carriage is deducted. Fine wool was grown in Spain in very early times, and there is a tradition that the ancestors of the " merino " sheep originally came from Britain, whence some derive their name from "Marino " owing to their having come by sea to Spain. A flock of sheep is said to have formed part of the dowry of John of Gaunt's daughter when she married the King of Castile. It is certain that at the beginning of the 15th century the finest wool was grown in Spain, where the poorness of the soil was favourable to the growth of fine hair and fibre, and it continued to take the first place until the advent of German wool deposed it under circumstances which will be narrated further on.

In early days the wool was spun and woven in the cottages, where, frequently, the whole family was engaged in one or other of these occupations, as in the illustration. The previous processes at the mill were the sorting, scouring and dyeing of the wool, unless the cloth was piece dyed or the wool was given out to a public dyer. The sorting will be best explained when we come to the German wool, as most of that from Spain arrived sorted or classed.

SCOURING.

The natural grease in the wool was first loosened by boiling in stale urine (it is now done by a chemical alkali made for the purpose) and then rinsed out in clean waters which came under considerable pressure into long trough, guarded by perforated zinc or copper ; a man stood on a platform in the middle and worked the wool about with a prong, by which means it came out clean and white. After the rinsing it was dried, and this was done in the strange round towers still to be seen in some places. Flues ran round these towers, and the wool was hung above them. There is a good specimen of one of these towers at Frogmarsh, and also one at Avening, now used as a cattle shed. They look rather like Martello towers, and may puzzle antiquarians in after times as to their object.

DYEING.

Dyeing was the next process. In order to get a good, permanent black, a foundation of blue is necessary, technically called " woading," from the fact that the vegetable woad was first used to produce it, and it continued to be employed in comparatively recent times, but, though still called woading, the dye now used is Indigo. Indigo is also a vegetable, grown principally in India, formerly worth, according to the season's crop, from 6s to 10s per lb., but of late years " synthetic indigo " has been invented, which gives almost as good a result at less than half the cost, and has consequently very much diminished the price of pure indigo and ruined the industry in India. Synthetic Indigo is a product of coal tar, and is said to have been first discovered by a Yorkshire-man, but the invention was improved by the Germans, and the trade in it has been captured by them. The process of producing this dye is a very expensive one, and the new industry was largely subsidised and protected by the German Government. One firm alone spent £1,000,000 on plant for making it. The absence of this dye has been a heavy loss to British Manufacturers, as no indigo of any sort can be bought under 12s a lb., and even at that price only in small quantities. It is earnestly to be hoped that the Royal Commission will be able to evolve some plan to enable it to be made profitably. Some measure of protection will be absolutely necessary, otherwise, when the War is over, the trade will go back to Germany, and all the capital spent on plants in this country will be lost.

The wool, having been dyed, was then picked by women on wire hurdles to free it from dye wares, lints and other foreign substances, after which it was necessary to open up or disentangle the locks and knots by carding.

CARDING.

Carding was formerly done by hand cards of wire, which must have been laborious and wearisome work. Carding or scribbling machines were not invented until the later years of the 18th century, and they must have been very different to the beautiful automatic machines of the present day, though they were a great saving of labour compared with the clumsy hand cards. The wool having been throughly mixed and disentangled was then ready for the next process of

SPINNING.

Wool was formerly spun in the cottages, as in the illustration, by the women and children, the men doing the heavier work of weaving. It must have been a most difficult task to get the yarn to the required pitch, and it was one man's work to ride round to the different cottages to inspect and weigh the yarn before it was allowed to be sent in or paid for at the mill. It was no uncommon thing for the spinning to be so badly done that it had to be chopped up again, the spinners, of course, receiving nothing for their work. This unsatisfactory state of things passed away towards the end of the 18th century owing to the invention of the " spinning Jenny," though it lingered on in some places till well into the 19th century. A few old spinning wheels are still preserved in the neighbourhood as curiosities, but they have long ceased to be used.

Spinning by machinery was first invented towards the middle of the 18th century by the son of a Huguenot refugee, Louis Paul, whose invention was improved by Richard Arkwright, and still further by Hargreaves. These machines were only adapted for spinning a few threads at a time, and were very different to the self-acting " Mules " of the present day, running hundreds of whirling spindles, and only requiring a girl to mend by hand any thread that happens to break, without stopping the machine.

After spinning, the chain was " warped " on an upright frame studded at each end with wooden pegs, the worker, usually a woman, walking backwards and forwards and hitching the chain on to the pegs at each end of the frame, joining it when necessary. The weft (locally called " abb "[1]) was also wound on to bobbins and the two were then ready for the loom. In the illustration, warping appears to be going on in a different manner, but I remember hand warping to have been done as above.

---

[1] The union of the abb and the warp passed into a local proverb. A man wishing to say he would make an end of a thing or a complete job of it would say ; " I'll make abb and warp of it."

Weaving.

Before the year 1796 two men were required to work a loom, one at each end, throwing the shuttle across to the other. This method must have been very clumsy and troublesome, and it had a special disadvantage in the fact that if one of the workers was at the public-house, not an uncommon occurrence with weavers, the other man was perforce idle and the loom earned no money. This difficulty was overcome by the introduction of the " fly shuttle," which enabled one man sitting in the middle to throw the shuttle from side to side by means of a string attached to a short handle. This was so great an improvement that it came rapidly into general use. The old system of weaving is still to be seen in some parts of the world. At Beyrout, in Syria, is a silk factory where beautiful materials are turned out entirely by manual labour, and there is not a wheel revolving by motive power in the whole place. The silk is wound from cocoons by children (alas ! some very young), spun on spinning wheels and woven on Jacquard looms, only that in this case three men are required to work the loom. One sits at each end and throws the shuttle across in the manner described above, and the man in the middle regulates the pattern and inserts when necessary gold and silver threads. The dyeing of the silk was done in pots. Altogether it was a very interesting example of the difficulties which must have occurred in the making of cloth before the introduction of machinery. Nevertheless, most beautiful silks were made at this factory, and probably the cloth turned out by manual labour in the olden time was equally satisfactory.

The loom is one of the oldest machines of man's invention. Flax or wool could be spun with the distaff, and later with the spinning wheel, but both would have been useless without the loom to weave the yarn into material. Allusions to weaving are common in the Bible and in the poets. Job says : " My days are swifter than a weaver's shuttle ; " the shaft of Goliath's spear was " like a weaver's beam," and there are many other instances. Shakespeare says : (All's Well that Ends Well, *Act* 4, *Sc.* 3)—

> " The web of our life is a mingled yarn, good and bad
> together ; "

Engrav'd for the Universal Magazine according to Act of Parlia

SPINNING, WEAVING, ETC. IN 1749

And Scott in Marmion :—

> " Oh what a tangled web we weave
> When first we practice to deceive."

Also Gray in " The Bard : "—

> " Weave the warp and weave the woof.
> The winding sheet of Edward's race."

The old power loom came into general use in 1836. It was only capable of weaving the simplest kind of cloth, and for certain sorts of plain material it is still hard to beat, but whereas the older looms could only throw one shuttle about 40 times a minute, the modern fast picking machines will throw two or three shuttles 100 times a minute and more for certain fabrics.

FULLING OR FELTING.

We now come to a process which is peculiar to wool. It has for its object the thickening of the ground of the cloth and rendering it firm and compact. In order to explain this process it is necessary to refer again to the peculiar structure of wool. If examined through the microscope it is found to consist of cones fitted into one another, having a jagged or serrated edge, and when subjected to many doublings and redoublings, and much pressure in the fulling process, and moistened with soap, these serrated edges and cones become entangled together, and when once knit to one another never lose their hold. Thus a cloth, when first off the loom, is flimsy and almost transparent, but after fulling becomes a firm compact material. Cloths lose considerably in length and width during the fulling process. In ancient times this was the only process necessarily carried on at the Mills, whence the felting of cloth is spoken of as " Milling," and the man who does the work is " The Millman."

The earliest form of fulling was probably effected by trampling on the cloth, and according to some, the common name of " Walker " owes its origin to this method of felting the cloth. Some such process was common in ancient times, and we read in the " Visions of Piers Plowman : "—

> " Cloth that cometh from the weaving is not
>   comely to wear
> Till it be fulled under fote or in fulling stocks
> Washen well with water and with tazels crached
> Touked and tevnted and under Tavlors hond."

From the above we conclude that fulling stocks were known in the time of Edward III., when the poem was written, and indeed they were in use long before that time. They were very familiar in later days, and I remember to have heard them going night and day and waking the echoes in the valleys. They were like gigantic wooden hammers, the heads weighing more than a hundredweight. The cloth was placed in the stock pits and the feet raised alternately and suffered to fall on it with great force, being lifted high by tappets fixed on a revolving shaft. It was a wonder how any cloth ever came out free from holes after being subjected to this hammering. It was a clumsy and dangerous machine, as it not infrequently happened that the workman fell into the stock pit whilst attending to the cloth, and in such cases he was lucky if he got out alive. The old stocks were superseded by a very much better machine called a " Fuller," which felts the cloth more perfectly and expeditiously. In the stocks an obstinate cloth was sometimes pounded for a whole week, but in the modern fuller it is seldom necessary to run a cloth for more than 12 hours. The fuller consists of a pair of revolving wheels, which draw the cloth sewn end to end like a jack towel, through a brass mouthpiece and force it under a weighted board, doubled and redoubled on itself. By the friction it becomes warm, and it is plentifully moistened with soap until the millman judges that he has got it to the right pitch. Then it is put into the washer for cleansing. The washer has two heavy iron or wooden rollers, between which the cloth passes, sewn as in the fuller, and it is run with cleansing materials until quite clean. Formerly many abominations, of which the least objectionable was pig's blood, were used, and old millmen will tell you that these horrors cleaned the cloth better than the chemicals now used.

Roughing or Dressing

I do not know how this process was carried out by hand, but the machine now used, called a " gig," is of considerable antiquity, and nothing has been found better for the work done by it than the teazle (*dipsacus fullorum*). Though in the coarser cloth wire is sometimes used, the natural teazle is almost universally employed in the finer products of the West of England. The teazle requires a stiff clay soil, and is a difficult and expensive crop to grow, but is very profitable in a good season. It is grown in Somersetshire, and formerly also in Gloucestershire, but the great majority come from France.

The teazles are fixed in small frames arranged round a large drum, which revolves rapidly, combing the face of the cloth to a soft long nap. Great judgment and delicacy of touch are required for this process,and it is easy to rough a cloth through and thus ruin it, especially if new and hard teazles are used in the early stages. I remember an old and very experienced rougher who always gardened in gloves in order to preserve his touch.

SHEARING.

The long nap raised by the teazle now requires to be shorn off, otherwise the cloth after a few days wear would present the appearance of a silk hat brushed the wrong way. The shearing was formerly done by hand shears, something like those used for shearing the sheep, the cloth being stretched over a sloping board. The grinding of those shears was quite an art and a separate trade, carried on where there was a small head of water sufficient to drive a grindstone. The remains of a pond used for this purpose may still be seen at the bottom of the Well Hill at Minchinhampton, and another near Nailsworth. The sign of the " Shears " was formerly common on public houses, and one still exists at Watledge, Nailsworth.

A great improvement in shearing was made about 1815 by Lewis, a Brimscombe manufacture, who invented what was called a " Cross Cutter," and took out a patent for his invention, which gave rise to a considerable amount of litigation in after years. The principle of the Cross Cutter was very similar to a lawn mowing machine at the present day. The cloth was stretched on a frame, and a cylinder with spiral blades traversed it from list to list. One section having been cut, the next was quickly stretched by boys, who became very expert in this work, and this continued until the whole cloth had been cut. This system, which was a great improvement on the clumsy hand shears, gave way in its turn to the " Perpetual," which is on the same principle as the Cross Cutter—that is, a spiral blade working on a straight edge—but with the important difference that in the Perpetual the

cloth is cut from end to end instead of in sections across it.
The adjusting of these machines is highly skilled work, and a
good foreman cutter or finisher deservedly earns high wages.
The fine cloth next went through the process of *potting*—*i.e.*,
rolling it tightly on an iron roller and immersing it in water
heated to about 150 degrees, by which means it is given a
permanent lustre. This process was also patented. In the
olden times the cloth was dried and stretched in racks in
the open air, in fair weather, and when the weather was not
favourable, in a long building heated by flues. This system
is now superseded by the tentering machine, in which the cloth
is stretched by means of small hooks to an even width, and
dried by passing over steam heated pipes. The cloth is then
sent to the warehouse, where it is pressed and packed ready
for sale.

We have now come to the finished cloth, and, although
there are many other processes more or less important, I hope
that this slight sketch will give an idea of the care and skill
required for the production of a piece of fine cloth, and that
those who possess a coat of such material will look upon it
with greater respect than they otherwise would.

In the next chapter I propose to return to the early days
of the firm of William Playne & Co., and to give an account
of the changes and vicissitudes through which it has passed.

William Playne
1772–1850

WILLIAM PLAYNE

CHAPTER XXII.

THE TRADES OF THE DISTRICT.

THE CLOTHING TRADE (*continued*).

THE records of the firm which survived the fire already mentioned, are somewhat confused and not easy to unravel. The accounts during the latter years of the 18th century are so mixed with personal and household expenses that they are difficult to disentangle, and moreover they are also intermixed with the accounts of a grist mill, which was run together with the cloth mill until the latter became very profitable, and the corn mill was given up.

The new business of Martha Playne and Son seems to have become remunerative at once, and soon recovered from the confusion left at Thomas Playne's death. The capital employed in the trade which on Nov. 1st, 1791, was £4,861, had increased in 1801 to over £12,000, and during that time the legacies left by Thomas Playne to his children had all been paid in full, though, at his death, there had not been enough to go round. William Playne had also built his new house, which is now the western wing of Longfords House.

The cloth made at Longfords consisted principally of superfine black and blue, single buff cassimeres, livery cloth, Spanish Stripes, etc. These Spanish Stripes, of which we shall have more to say later on, were so called because they were made of Spanish wool, and had a stripe in the list or selvage. They were bought by the merchants for export to China, but the trade had not at this time attained to the important position it occupied when taken up by the East India Company. It was a rather flimsy material with very little dress on it, and of an immense variety of colours, which, as the cloths were all piece dyed, must have been most difficult to get even and perfect with the dyeing materials then in use.

No records survive of any large purchases of Spanish wool before the year 1809. In that year Napoleon closed all the ports of the continent to British trade, thinking by such means to deal a deadly blow to British credit and prosperity, his plans for the invasion of England having been shattered by Nelson at Trafalgar. This attempt to destroy British commerce proved a complete failure, but, nevertheless, while the me-bargo lasted prices of all commodities went up by leaps and bounds, and wool rose to unprecedented prices. Whether by accident, or foresight, the firm held a large stock of Spanish wool, and, whilst still keeping the mill going, the partners were able to sell the surplus at huge prices, thus making a large profit. On January 11th, 1809, there is an invoice of 77 bags of wool sold by the firm at prices ranging from 9s 6d to 11s 6d per lb., according to quality, the total amount of the invoice being £8,650. On February 7th, there is another invoice for a still larger amount, at prices ranging from 16s 6d to 18s per lb. In March the prices mounted higher, and there is a letter from London merchants saying that Spanish wool had changed hands at no less a price than 23s to 23s 6d per lb., and none was to be had under 22s. The natural consequence was that the price of cloth also rose with that of wool, and manufacturers were forced to raise their prices by 3s to 4s 6d per yard, and as the scarcity of wool increased, by 6s to 8s a yard. On January 19th, the following letter was received from a London house :—" We wish you to send us, soon as you can, as under, at as low a price as you can afford, not to exceed an advance of 6s a yard, and believe you will act liberally to us, and we shall act the same to you." Another dated August 5th, complains that 50 pieces had not been delivered, and continues :—" We hope that you will not charge us so high as 28s 6d for blacks, and pray don't be so anxious after riches, and recollect that we took of you when you could not sell." It would be refreshing to receive a few letters like the above at the present time !

The profits made by these transactions in wool, and the enhanced price of cloth were very large, and the business was considerably extended owing to the East India Co. coming into the market as buyers of Spanish Stripe, large contracts being offered by them for competition. This necessitated larger manufacturing premises, and therefore the buildings at

Longfords were considerably increased, and other mills also were built, notably one at Horsley, now pulled down, but of which remains are still to be seen.

The increase in the output of the firm necessitated a correspondingly large increase in the amount of wool bought. In 1816 there occurs a statement of account, showing purchases of Spanish wool amounting to the value of £41,331 12s 8d, and another in 1817 to £35,871 11s, in addition to other records of large purchases.

Besides the large quantity of stripe made under contract for the East India Co., the regular trade was also extended, and in times of great activity wool was given out to other manufacturers to be spun and woven, and in some cases finished. It was sometimes necessary to divide out a part of the larger East India Co.'s orders so as to deliver them up to time, the original contracting firm being always held responsible for their punctual delivery. It sometimes happened that a large number of cloths were rejected, but by diplomacy and allowances matters were usually accommodated. The pieces of cloth for the East India Co. had to be of a uniform length of 36 yards, 58½ inches wide, and to weigh 34 lbs. The largest contract of which I have a record is for 10,000 pieces, but I believe there were some for an even larger amount. The East India Co. consigned the bulk of these stripes to " How Qua," a merchant in Canton, in a very large way, and I believe they were all sold in China. The bales were sealed with the family crest, an oak tree, and this mark came to be so well-known that the bales so sealed passed without question. The marks however, were forged after a time, and the immunity from examination ceased.

The following is a notice of a Warrant having been passed for payment at the Bank of England for Spanish Stripe bought by the East India Co. :—

> Mr Simons presents his Compliments to
> Messrs. William and Peter Playne and this
> day passed a Warrant

For White Spanish Stripe Cloths	£11,800	0	0
Dyed Spanish Stripe Cloths	12,735	16	1
	£24,535	16	1

Office of Buying and Warehouse
East India House, 1st October, 1828.

These periodical payments were paid in one cheque on the Bank of England.

We must go back to the year 1806, when the great enterprise of the creation of Longfords Lake was accomplished. Before this, the only storage of water was the present lower pond of comparatively small size. Water power was at that time a most valuable asset, for the steam engine had not come into general use, and water was, and still is, the cheapest motive power. The brothers conceived the idea of damming up the water of the main stream and many springs which fed it. It was a great work, and many days and nights of thought there must have been before the final decision was made. The dam is 150 yards long, and about 30 feet high, and the area of the lake was formerly 15 acres, but it has been much silted up at the upper end, which takes 2 or 3 acres off its original size. In places it has a depth of 26 feet, and is still a fine sheet of water. In order to pen this water in it was necessary to overflow some of Philip Sheppard's land, which was purchased for £400, a peppercorn rent of 2s 6d being reserved, which, however, was, I believe, never demanded or paid. I have been told by those, long since dead, who remember the construction of the dam, that a high wide dry wall was built, against which on both sides clay was puddled. The inner face of the dam was also clayed, and the outer covered with earth. The dam has never hitherto given any trouble, but the brothers had not complete confidence in their work, and did not venture to build their new mills across the valley. They therefore cut a canal of considerable length, which brought the water to the mills, built at right angles to the lake, and well away from the direct line of the flow of the water in case of the bursting of the dam. Although the dam has given no trouble, the canal constantly requires repair, and has been a perpetual expense to keep in order. The total cost of the dam, exclusive of the canal, was £945, not a high price for a work of that size. During the filling of the new lake very little water was allowed to go down stream, and actions were threatened by every mill-owner in the valley. But it was represented that the storage of so large a quantity would be very useful in dry seasons, and the opposition was gradually withdrawn, and the lake allowed to fill without further trouble. It was for many years a noted place for trout fishing, as the

EAST VIEW OF LONGFORDS

fish grew to a great size on the new bottom, but unfortunately someone was ill-advised enough to put in roach, which increased so rapidly that ultimately it was necessary to put in pike to keep them down.

During the machine breaking riots the dam was guarded day and night, as it was proposed by the rioters to cut it through and sweep away the mills and machinery. Immense damage might have been done had the attempt not been frustrated.

Notwithstanding the advantage of a large storage of water, steam engines were early in use at Longfords. Some of the earlier contracts with Boulton and Watt have not survived, and the first I have is dated 1815. The cost, without fixing or carriage, and also in addition to some accessories, was £970 for an engine of 20 h.p. Boulton and Watt at this time had almost a monopoly in the making of beam engines, but in subsequent transactions, in 1823 and 1826, competition had materially reduced the price. Three of these engines were going at Longfords, and one at the Iron Mills in my recollection, and one of the early ones was only scrapped three years ago.

The first invoice of German wool to any large extent which I have been able to discover is dated Jan. 24th, 1808, and was for 235 bales sold by March & Ebsworth, of London, " for their principals," at prices ranging from 4s to 6s 3d per lb., and the total is £15,359 9s 6d. From this time onward more German and less Spanish wool was used at Longfords. The imports from Spain gradually dwindled, and in a few years ceased altogether, the Spanish wool not being able to compete with the far finer German wool. The first flock of merino sheep introduced into Germany was presented by the King of Spain to the Elector of Saxony, about 1760, the poor and sandy soil of some parts of Saxony proving eminently suitable for the growth of fine-haired, short stapled wool. There were other importations of sheep from Spain, notably in 1778, and so much care was taken and so much judgment used in crossing that, before long, they far outstripped their Spanish ancestors in fineness of fleece, and became famous as the " Electoral breed." The great demand for German wool stimulated its production until the fine wool merino sheep spread over the greater part of Saxony, Silesia,

East and West Prussia, Poland and Moravia, and ultimately to Hungary.

In the year 1824, William Playne, junior, made his first journey to Germany to buy wool in the place where it was grown, and in this enterprise he was the pioneer whose example was later on followed by other manufacturers. In these early days there were no wool fairs such as came later into existence, and the wool had to be bought at the various country houses, where Mr Playne and his broker were most hospitably entertained by the proprietors, who farmed their own estates, and took great pride in keeping up the quality of their sheep. The distance by road from Calais to Dresden was 850 miles, and Breslau some 200 miles farther. William Playne used to keep a carriage at Calais and drive all the way, and very monotonous and wearisome the journeys must have been, and the annoyance was increased by the examination of the luggage at the frontier of every little petty state before the establishment of the Zollverein. It frequently happened that the luggage was unloaded and examined twice in one day. In one of these journeys, William Playne, senior, accompanied his son, and there are some very interesting letters which he wrote home describing the country he passed through, the state of agriculture, the wages of the workmen in town and country, the state of education, etc.

Silesian wool soon came to the fore, and the great wool fair at Breslau was established, to which, in the early part of June, all the wool from the neighbourhood, and also from long distances, of sometimes two or three days' journey, was brought in by wagon and deposited in the streets and squares of the old city, or else in the warehouses of the Jews, who drove a very lucrative trade by lending money to the farmers and proprietors and taking the wool as security.

WOOL SORTING.

The Spanish wool did not need much sorting, being already classed in Spain, but the sorting of German wool was a very skilled and elaborate process. There were usually five sorts in the finer German wool, called in most mills 1st, 2nd, and so on according to quality. At Longfords the names were, and still are, RRR (treble R), RR (double R), R, F & T, besides " short coarse," or list. These names originated in the time of the Spanish wools ; F signifies " finos," or fine, " Ra-finos," very fine, " Tertias," or thirds. The German wool, being much finer, necessitated other names, and hence RR and RRR.

The sorter stands surrounded by large baskets with a wire hurdle in front of him, on which he spreads the fleece, the head to the left and the tail to the right. A glance tells him the quality of the bulk of the fleece, and knowing where to look for the different qualities he proceeds to " break " it. The finest wool on the sheep grows on the middle of the back, on the belly, and on the forelegs, the coarser on the breech, the neck, and the top of the head. These the sorter breaks off and throws into the proper baskets and the bulk into another, according to quality. It sometimes happened, but not often, that all five sorts were found on one fleece. The sheep which grew this wool were strange looking animals, very leggy, and with a very naked appearance. The small quanity of wool which they grew, sometimes 1½ to 2 lbs. weight after they were washed, rendered them very delicate, and, during the severe winters in those parts, they were housed in barns and fed largely on rye and other dry food. The ryebeards were a very great nuisance, as, notwithstanding all the processes for getting rid of foreign matter, they still appeared on the face of the cloth, necessitating a whole army of " pickers " with tweezers, whose operations did not add to the beauty of the face of the cloth. This difficulty is now a thing of the past, as the cloth is passed through a bath containing a solution composed chiefly of chloride of aluminum, which kills vegetable without affecting animal matter, and, after being baked at a temperature of 240 degrees Fahrenheit, the filth easily shakes out. Some manufacturers prefer to " pickle " the wool in a weak solution of sulphuric acid before dyeing. The German wool gradually decreased in quality owing to the carcase of the sheep becoming more valuable than the wool. New mutton-producing breeds were introduced, and, at the present time, very little fine wool comes from the countries which formerly produced it in such large quantities. The wool now used at Longfords is almost exclusively Australian, exported in the grease, of the first clothing quality. The merino sheep was originally introduced into Australia from the Cape in the beginning of the 19th century, and, by the continued importation of the best blood from the continent of Europe, the wool has attained a high degree of excellence both for clothing and for combing. The importation of Australian wool at the present time is enormous. In 1913 the importations for the year reached no less than 2,296,000 bales, of the total value of about 20 million pounds sterling.

In the years between 1836 and 1848 the profits of the firm gradually diminished. It was a transition period ; the stripe trade was dead, and competition, especially with Yorkshire, which was rapidly rising in importance as a manufacturing centre, was very keen. In 1848 however, a change of fashion again brought the fine West of England Cloth into prominence, and then began the palmy days of the trade in the Stroud valleys. All the mills now silent or devoted to other trades were working to their utmost capacity, producing the famous Broad Cloth, which had so great a vogue for many years, not only in our own country, but also on the Continent and in America. No firm had a greater reputation for producing this Cloth than William Playne & Co., whose whole output was frequently sold as soon as it was finished to the large wholesale houses in London, in Manchester, and in Scotland. This prosperity lasted for about 40 years, when the fashion again changed ; the old broad cloth gradually disappeared, and cheaper materials were demanded. The superfine blue cloth for naval uniforms is still made to a considerable extent, but the black is seldom asked for.

Towards the end of the year 1910, it became evident that the old four-storey Mill Buildings at Longfords were no longer safe for the modern heavy and quick-running machinery. The workshops in these old buildings were very low, scarcely more than 10 feet high, and the floors, moreover, were so saturated with oil and caked with grease that, had a fire occurred during working hours, those who were in the upper storeys of the old Mill might have had some difficulty in escaping. The outside walls, also, which had stood for more than a century, began to show signs of the heavy strain to which they had been subjected by the new machinery, and in all probability before long the Factory Inspector might have condemned them.

It became an anxious consideration, therefore, whether the Mills should be closed and the business given up, or whether

SPINNING MILL AT LONGFORDS, 1914

a very large outlay should be incurred by re-building the greater part of the Mill and in re-arranging the position of the machinery. Perhaps this outlay was not justified by the state of the business at that time. But the closing of the Mill, with all that it would involve, was a disaster which no one liked to contemplate, and the necessary work was therefore decided on.

The great difficulty of building on any large scale was due to the narrowness of the valley, which was already occupied by large buildings, and the problem was where to place another still larger, near enough to the power to be run in conjunction with those that were still in good condition. According to modern ideas, it is advisable to place as much as possible of the heavy machinery on the ground floor, thereby giving greater stability, causing less vibration, and, in the case of a shed, reducing the risk of fire to a minimum.

After much consideration, and after examining several possible and impossible sites for the new building, only one seemed likely to be satisfactory, and though involving double the cost that would have been necessary if it had been possible to build on an ordinary foundation, yet it was open to less objection than other suggested sites. The decision, therefore, ultimately come to was to build the new shed over the middle pond, but on driving some experimental piles into the bed of this pond, the subsoil was found to be so marshy that no ordinary piling would have been of the slightest use.

By the advice of Mr Robert Stotesbury, of Stonehouse, who was the Engineer and Architect of the building, ferro-concrete piles of large size were used. These piles were 18 feet long and 12 inches square, the bottom ends being pointed and shod with iron. They were made in square moulds, the steel core being completely covered with concrete. When sufficiently solid to be taken out of the moulds, they were allowed from one to two months to dry out completely, according to the weather. They were then driven into the bed of the pond at regular intervals by a steam "Monkey," weighing about a ton, until they came to a solid foundation on the Lias clay below. On these piles reinforced concrete beams, $13'' \times 7''$, of similar construction were fixed, and, finally, a floor, also of ferro-concrete, $3''$ thick. No timber was used, except for scaffolding, and on this foundation the brick shed was built. It is 160 feet long and 85 feet in width, and even when all the machinery is running but little vibration is felt. A date stone, on which is carved the family crest (an Oak Tree), with the motto " Reviresco," records that it was laid by Mrs Playne, March 1, 1912, and by the beginning of August in the same year the building had been finished and looms were running.

The building of this shed enabled a re-arrangement of the workshops to be made, by which all the heavier machinery was brought down to the ground floor. In the illustration part of a new Spinning Mill is seen, in which are four self-acting " Mules," each containing 420 spindles, and only requiring the attention of a girl to mend any yarn that may happen to break, without stopping the machine. The whole Mill is run by electric power, except the Fullers and Washers, which are driven by water. The electricity is supplied from a central power station, the current being conveyed from the dynamo to motors in the various workshops. It is a much cleaner and neater system than the cumbersome cogwheels of former days, and the loss of power by friction is very much less. All the machinery now used in Longfords Mills is thoroughly up-to-date, and capable of turning out more cloth than at any time during the last fifty years.

The demand for fine West of England Broadcloth gradually dwindled, and finally ceased altogether ; and though some of the older generation continued for some years to use it, very little was made after the year 1890, and it is now seldom asked for.

Superfine Blue Cloths, together with other makes of blue for Naval purposes are still in demand, but, with the extinction of the old black Broadcloth, it was, of course, necessary to make other materials which were more fashionable, and for which there was a readier sale, to take its place.

A great variety of cloth is now turned out at Longfords, such as Beavers, Venetians, Serges, Tweeds, Worsted Coatings, Tropicals, &c., &c., and there is also a large trade in a great variety of fancy flannel suitings. No doubt there are other materials which will be made when the taste of the public demands them, and Longfords Mills are well equipped for supplying them when they come along. Since the War began,

WEAVING SHEDS, LONGFORDS, 1914

the Mills have been running, sometimes overtime, on Khaki and Naval Uniform cloth of all kinds, though in the case of the latter the shortage of the Indigo supply, already mentioned, makes a difficulty.

I am now come to the end of this sketch of the Clothing Trade, in which I have been engaged now for 50 years. We believe that there is still a future before the old business, and, supported by our workpeople, we trust that the day is far distant when Longfords Mills will have to be closed.

With very few exceptions, all the Mills which formerly worked to their utmost capacity in producing the West of England Broadcloth are now devoted to a great variety of other trades. From Avening the clothing business has entirely disappeared ; of the two Mills formerly worked there, one is now a Flour Mill, and the other, which stood near the old Rectory, and was called " George's Mill," has, within recent years, been pulled down. In Nailsworth several of the old Mills have disappeared, and the one left has been greatly enlarged, and now produces " leatherboards." The large Mills at Dunkirk are used for several purposes—hosiery, stick works, and the metal furniture for umbrellas. Some have taken to making flock for bedding, and at Dyehouse is a large and flourishing Brass Foundry. Thus the only Mills within the ancient Parish of Minchinhampton still working on woollen cloth are those of Messrs. William Playne & Co. at Longfords, and of Messrs. P. C. Evans & Co., of Brimscombe. There are some large Woollen Mills in other parishes, notably those of Messrs. Strachan & Co. at Lodgemore, Messrs. Apperley, Curtis & Co. at Dudbridge, and Messrs. Marling & Co. at King Stanley. There is also a large Mill at Eastington, and also at Cam, where cloth is still made. On the whole, though some of us may regret the decline of the old broadcloth, yet we must recognise that the new industries have done much to restore prosperity to the district.

CHAPTER XXIII.

MINCHINHAMPTON CHURCHWARDENS'
ACCOUNTS

NO History of Minchinhampton would be complete without a mention of the accounts of the Churchwardens, which are of great interest. Since they were transcribed by the late Mr John Bruce, Treasurer of the Society of Antiquaries, in 1854, and published in "Archæologia" (Vol. xxxv., pp. 409-452), extracts have frequently been published in the Parish Magazine and elsewhere. The accounts begin in 1555—that is, in the second year of the reign of Philip and Mary.

The ordinary ancient revenue of the Churchwardens, as shown in these accounts, was derived from the following sources :—1. The payment from Rodborough.[1]   2. The profit from underletting a Church House and other houses, and of a piece of land held under a lease from the Lord of the Manor. 3. "Hogling Money," which Mr Bruce considers to have been a customary payment by the sheep farmers of the parish for their hoglings or hoggets—that is, their sheep of the second year. This payment was discontinued in 1595. 4. Paschal Money, which was a customary contribution by parishioners who came "to take their rights"—that is, to confess, be absolved and receive the Eucharist at Easter. 5. An annual collection made by the Churchwardens from house to house throughout the Parish ; many contributed not in money but in kind, a large amount of wheat and malt being thus accumulated. The last item in the receipts is the profit

---

[1] Before the building of the Church of Rodborough, an Aisle in the Mother Church was set apart for the accommodation of the People of Rodborough for which a payment of 20s. per annum was made.

from Church Ale, brewed by the Churchwardens from the donations in kind. A feast was held at the Church House at Whitsuntide, when the Church Ale was sold to all comers, and the day passed in revels and rural sports. From this source the Churchwardens made a profit of £3 to £5 every year.

Space will only allow a few typical extracts of these accounts to be given, and probably there are many copies of Mr Bruce's transcript still in existence for those who desire to study the whole.

The first entry of receipts is as follows :—

> This ys the accompte off Jhon Cambryg and Andrewe Haward, churche wardens off Hampton, mayde in the seconde yere off Kyeng P. and M. In the yere off our lorde God M.ccccc.lv.

Then follow various sums received for rent.

The summe of thys, v li. j d.

A long list of payments for the same year, a few of which are as follows :—

Item, for vij li. off wax to make the pascall taper, the faunt taber and makyng, vij s. iij d.

> for smoke farthyng, x d.
> to Spennell for makyng off the sepulkyer, xij d.
> for drynkyns a good ffryday, iiij d.
> to Sir Roger for to bokys, ij s. vj d.
> for a pyxe, iij s. x d.
> for frankynesenns, j d.
> at the wysytacyonn, ij s. iiij d.

Item, we mayd off owr ale and ester monye, iij li. xij d.

> The sume off owr charges ys, v li. xviij s. iij d.

In the following year (1556) the titles given to Philip and Mary are interesting.

> oʳ Soŭayne [Lord] and Ladye Phillippe and Marie, by the grace of God kynge and quene of England, Fraunce, Naples, Jerusalem, and Irelande, Defendours of the Faith, Princes of Spayne and Sycyll, Archedukes of Austrie, Dukes of myllayne, burgundye and brabant, Countyeȝ of haspurge, Flaunders and tyroll.

Every year occur the payment of 20s from Rodborough,

and hoglyng money, and also the various payments at the
" vysytacion."

These visitations occurring, as they did, every few months,
were very onerous and expensive to the Churchwardens and
parishioners. On this subject Mr Bruce says : " The people
were not merely superintended, but were teased and irritated
by perpetual visitations and inquiries, often about trifles.
They were compelled to go to Tetbury, to Stroud, to Painswick, to Gloucester, to Cirencester, and, in turn, three or
four times a year to most of the surrounding towns. And
all these visitations were attended by fees to the Paritor or
summoning officer, one of the most unpopular of public func-
tionaries. He travelled round from parish to parish, taking
with him, besides his summons, which he was paid for de-
livering, a book of articles, or a brief, or a proclamation, or
something or other, which was also to be paid for. At the
day appointed the Churchwardens and sidesmen were bound
to attend personally. They had to deliver returns often, as
stated in these accounts, of " none recusants," but which
they were bound to get written for them by some paid scribe,
and which were, of course, not received or filed without payment of fees to the officers of the Court. The parish also
had to pay the travelling expenses of the persons representing
it on these occasions, and the Churchwardens were not infrequently called upon to purchase a copy of a new edition
of some ecclesiastical book, which it was generally found
economical to buy, as refusal was sure to be remembered,
and sometimes to be followed by citation or excommunication on some pretext or other, as, for instance, " Paid for
takinge off our excommunication for not appearing when we
were summoned, 6s 8d." As time went on these exactions
became more and more onerous. In 1635, for example,
there is an entry of a journey to Tetbury, when fees amounting
to £1 2s 7d were paid, and

> for makeinge a terriall of the glibe lands, and caringe
> it in, 3 s. 5 d. ; at Gloucester court, for expences and fees,
> 3 s. 2 d. ; the 2ᵈ tyme, for expences and fees, 4 s. 6 d. ;
> the 3rd tyme, for expences and fees, 1 s. 7 d. ; the 4th
> tyme, for expences and fees, and the sydesmens charges
> there, 9 s. 4 d. ; the 5th tyme, for expences and fees,
> 4 s. 4 d. ; at visitation, the 17th November, 12 s. 1 d. ;
> to the vissitor of the Church, 5 s,

making a total of £3 6s 0d, which would represent a much larger sum in these days. Thus these unfortunate Church-wardens were compelled, in one year, to make a journey to Tetbury, five journeys to Gloucester, besides a visitation of their Church, entailing fresh expenses. It was no wonder that the Church of England and Episcopal government declined in popularity, owing largely to these perpetual imposts and over-watchful superintendence, especially under James I. and Charles I.

On the accession of Queen Mary, the parishioners of Minchinhampton, who do not seem to have much favoured the Reformation, reverted with alacrity to the old religion. A Breviary was bought in 1555. Sir Roger the Priest was allowed 2s 6d for other books, and one Pockmore was also paid " for a boke 2s " in 1558. A Porthose (Breviary) cost 15d. Priestly vestments were provided at little cost. A carefully-preserved cope was mended at an expense of 12d; a Rood cost xxs. a Tabernacle 12s. and a pyx 3s 10d, and two surplices were also renovated at a cost of 3s 4d.

> For " Frankynegsens v j d.; for waxe to make the pastall taper and the fownt taper vj s.; for mayng the tapers off the Awter iij d.; for mendyng off the horgons xij d.; for mayng off the sepulkeyer, xij d.; for watchyng off the same xij d."

Thus provided, Easter seems to have been celebrated with all the old fashioned pomp, but a change came over the scene, though very slowly, soon after the accession of Queen Elizabeth. Then, in 1576, the following accounts appear.

> Our charges at the Archebusshoppe of Canterburye3 vysytacyone at Payneswyck, ij s. ix d. ; for a book of artycle3, vj d. ; for Pentecost money, otherwyse peter pence, sometyme payed to Antecryst of Roome, xvj d. ; for a booke of Commone prayer, v s. ; for ryngenge the daye of the Quene3 maiestye3 enterynge unto the crowne, whome God longe tyme wee beseche to preserue, ix d. ; for aunswerynge the parishe mattere before the Com-myssoneres, iiij s. ; payed and dysbursed for aunswerynge dyuerse faulse vntrothe3 suggested by Wylliam Halle, Thomas Kembridge, John Hallydaye, John Sandelle, and Richard mallard, to the sayd Commyssyoneres, vj s. viij d.

Notwithstanding the above, the Reformation did not make rapid progress at Minchinhampton. The parishioners seem to have been of a conservative disposition, and did not at once accommodate themselves to the new state of things ; and there were also two other reasons which tended to delay the change. The second Lord Windsor was a staunch supporter of Queen Mary, and the Rector of Minchinhampton, appointed by him, was the celebrated Gilbert Bourne who had the temerity to defame Edward VI. and extol Bishop Bonnor in a sermon at Paul's Cross, which so enraged the populace that he was barely saved from their violence by the intervention of Bradford and Rogers, the subsequent Martyrs, one of whom caught the dagger aimed at Bourne. Thus, whilst Bishop Hooper was doing his utmost to bring Protestantism to Gloucester, Bourne was doing all he could to keep it away from Minchinhampton. Bourne kept a Curate, who is alluded to in the accounts as " Sir Roger," and he, no doubt, followed in the footsteps of his Rector, who probably seldom came to Hampton after his appointment as Bishop of Bath and Wells by Queen Mary.

A change came with the appointment of the next Rector, Thomas Freeman. A Bible of the new translation was bought, and a desk was erected at the pulpit, the prayers having previously been read at the altar. There is also a payment of 6s 8d " to John Mayo and John Lyth for pullinge down, destroying, and throwing out of the Church sundry superstitious things tending to the maintenance of idolatry." But it was not till 1594 that the Church was entirely purged of its idolatory, as in that year appears an entry " Paid : for a precept to Remoue the woman out of the churche porche." This was presumably a statue of the Virgin Mary.

There are numberless entries of payments for killing certain animals considered to be mischievous. The heads of foxes, otters, " grayes " (badgers) were paid at the rate of 1s each. Hedgehogs fetched 6d, and a bat's legs the same. Later on kites, jays and magpies were also paid for at varying rates. The entries on this subject in the accounts are innumerable.

The name of Lord Windsor in several generations occurs very frequently, and many other members of the family, sometimes under the name of " Mr Walter Wyndsor, Esquire."

The last Lord Windsor gave the sum of £10 towards the new casting of the Bells, which gift is thus recorded :—

" I doe give out of my rents of minchinhampton, to bee payd by my bailife of that maner att the next receipt, toward the mackinge and new castinge of the belles in y^t churche, the some of ten pound ; in wittnesse whereof, I have sett to my hand this 15th day of May, 1633."

THOMAS WINDESOR.

In connection with Lord Windsor there is a well-known story related by Dugdale on the authority of the above Thomas Lord Windsor, the reference to which is given by Mr Bruce as " Baronage 308."[1]

" The family of Windsor had been seated for many generations at Stanwell, between Staines and Colnbrook, a situation which possessed the great advantages of contiguity to the metropolis and to Windsor. Henry VIII. thought their residence too near the latter place. He sent Lord Windsor a message that he would dine with him, and at the appointed time his Majesty arrived, and was received with bountiful and loyal hospitality. On leaving Stanwell, Henry addressed his host in words which breathe the very spirit of Ahab. He told Lord Windsor " that he liked so well of that place that he resolved to have it, yet not without a more beneficial exchange." Lord Windsor answered that he hoped his Highness was not in earnest. He pleaded that Stanwell had been the seat of his ancestors for many ages, and begged that His Majesty would not take it from him. The King replied that it must be so. With a stern countenance, he commanded Lord Windsor, upon his allegiance, to go speedily to the Attorney-General, who should more fully acquaint him with the royal pleasure. Lord Windsor obeyed his imperious master, and found the draught ready made of a conveyance, in exchange for Stanwell, of lands in Worcestershire and Gloucestershire, and amongst them of the impropriate rectory of Minchinhampton, with the Manor and a residence adjoining the town. Lord Windsor submitted to the enforced banishment, but it broke his heart. Being ordered to quit Stanwell immediately, he left there the provisions laid

1 Dugdale's *Baronage of England*, 1675-6, ii. 307-9.

in for the keeping of his wonted Christmas hospitality, declaring, with a spirit more prince-like than the treatment he had received, that " they should not find it Bare Stanwell."

If he passed his Christmas in his new residence at Minchinhampton he probably found it bare enough. He died in the following March.

CHAPTER XXIV.

THE MINCHINHAMPTON VESTRY MINUTES

B ESIDES the Churchwardens' accounts, the Vestry Minutes of Minchinhampton, beginning about 1786, are also very interesting. The little town and parish appear to have been well and successfully governed by our fore-fathers, and the Minutes show the care with which all questions coming before them were discussed and settled. The names of some of the most regular attendants at these Meetings are still familiar among us, and their descendants also take their part in such local affairs as are left for them to manage.

By the kindness of Mr and Mrs Sidney Webb, I am allowed to quote from their great work on " English Local Government " the following description of the business trans-acted by the Minchinhampton Vestry :—

[1] Such a quasi-voluntary local government is well seen in the records of Minchinhampton—an unincor-porated ancient town, and centre of the old-fashioned Gloucestershire Woollen Industry. The Minutes in the latter part of the eighteenth century reveal to us the Vestry meeting monthly to relieve the poor, repair the Church, and mend the roads. But we gather that at all these routine meetings, the " Vestry " consists only of the two or three Churchwardens and Overseers, other inhabi-tants only attending when the business personally con-cerned them. Thus the Rector, far from presiding by right of his office, only appears at long intervals, once to protest against a proposed removal of the Pound, and another time to sign a resolution, along with the principal tithe payers, by which the Parish agreed to exonerate his tithes from rates during his whole life, on condition

1 History of English Local Government, pp. 54-55.

that he accepted a fixed composition. The half-a-dozen manufacturers do not bestir themselves to attend at all, until the high rates of 1800 incite them to discuss ways and means, and to resist the proposed new assessment of their mills. And here and there throughout the Minute Book, the attendance of this or that substantial ratepayer appears only when he comes to bargain with the Parish about the sum he will agree to pay for exoneration from his liability to maintain a bastard child. What is perhaps more significant is the evidence, during a whole generation, of the constant desire of the parish officers to fortify themselves in every important step, not merely by the legally authoritative resolution of a duly convened Vestry, but by the actual presence and signed agreement of all the principal inhabitants. Whenever the " Vestry " is about to " make, adjust and finish " a rate, embark on legal proceedings, raise men for the Militia, or revise the discipline and dietary of the Workhouse, the meeting is habitually adjourned, and the inhabitants of the Parish are specially summoned to the adjourned meeting and " earnestly requested to attend so that the general sense of the parish may be known upon the business." On one occasion, when the Parish officers were driven to re-organise the whole Poor Law administration of their little kingdom, they plaintively urge, in their notice, that no plan will " succeed unless gentlemen of character and ability in the Parish take an active part in the parochial concerns so as to give a regular and vigorous attention at stated times."

The Master of the Workhouse received, besides his keep, a salary of 15 guineas, subsequently increased to 20 guineas, and later still to 25. Besides the master and matron, there was the contractor, who " farmed " the inmates at certain rates, which at Minchinhampton do not seem to have erred on the side of extravagance. There were many other servants of the Parish, chief among whom was the Parish Clerk,[1] "holding an immemorial freehold office, half-way between that of a Curate, or assistant Minister and that of a Church menial." His appointment rested either with the incumbent or with the inhabitants in vestry assembled, where it sometimes became the subject of dispute. At Minchinhampton he was

WEST VIEW OF LONGFORDS

appointed by the Rector and licensed by the Chancellor of the Diocese, but to the office of Vestry Clerk, which he also usually held, he was appointed by the Vestry itself, which body also paid his salary.

Another important officer was the Sexton, or Sacristan, appointed in Minchinhampton up to 1825 by the Rector and Churchwardens, but afterwards by the Vestry. Mr and Mrs Webb say that the office of Sexton was not uncommonly held by a woman. There is no mention of a Beadle, but he was a very usual functionary, as was also the Hayward, who, in Minchinhampton, has from time immemorial been appointed by the Court Leet of the Manor. Another amazing Parish officer is mentioned by Mr and Mrs Webb, though he does not occur in Minchinhampton, who acted as " Dog Whipper," and kept quiet during Divine Service the dogs which members of the congregation brought with them to Church. This official was armed with a whip and a wand " for the quieting of the children during Divine Service, as well as for whipping out of the dogs." An instance is mentioned where the dogs " from the Hall " were allowed a special pew where they were exempt from the attention of the dog whipper.

In 1799 a Committee was appointed to consider the affairs of the Parish, probably on account of the great increase of the Poor Rate, and in 1800 the report of the Committee was presented and adopted by the Vestry, when it was " unanimously resolved that for the management of the Parish concerns a General Board should be appointed consisting of twenty-five gentlemen, which Board should meet about once a quarter and the Churchwardens and Overseers for the time being shall be considered as Members of the Board ; at these quarterly meetings, they shall audit the accounts, order the payment of bills, confirm or rescind the rules of the weekly visiting committee, hereafter mentioned, and fix the assessment to be levied on the Parish."

The little community continued thus to govern itself until the passing of the Poor Law Amendment Act in 1834 deprived the Parishes of the greater part of their functions. A Commission appointed in 1832 to enquire into the administration of the Poor Law by the Parish Vestries led to the Act of 1834 and the grouping of Parishes for Poor Law purposes into Unions under one central authority, to which each Parish contributed its guardians, elected by plural voting according to the amount at which each voter was rated. Under a rateable value of £50 one vote only was allowed, and every £25 in addition carried another up to the number of six votes. Most of the landowners possessed the full maximum number, and all Justices of the Peace were also ex-officio guardians. This undemocratic form of election, known as the Sturges Bourne Acts, was not carried without considerable opposition, especially in Lancashire and Yorkshire, where Vestry Meetings frequently ended in riots. Another of the principal causes of the decline in the authority of the Vestry was the opposition to the Church rate by the Nonconformists and Roman Catholics, who adopted a very effective method, known within recent years as " passive resistance." The means for the recovery of Church rates were cumbersome, especially in the case of the larger amounts, where an action in the ecclesiastical courts was necessary, or, if the amount did not exceed £10, the amount was recoverable before two Justices of the Peace, sitting in Petty Sessions. Compulsory Church Rates were finally abolished in 1868, though they had long before this time fallen into disuse. Vestry Meetings are still held in country districts, but only once a year, usually at Easter, and the duties being merely nominal, are seldom attended by any parishioner except the Parish officials.

CHAPTER XXV.

HIGHWAYS AND ROADS

I MUST in this Chapter also express my thanks to Mr and Mrs Sidney Webb for kindly allowing me to make use of their " Story of the King's Highway," a portion of their larger work on " English Local Government," from which I take the following extract :—

[1] The earliest highways in England of which there is any sign are the ancient trackways—sometimes first marked out by passing animals—which were used by the British inhabitants. These ancient lines of traffic were probably irregular and winding, and frequently worn below the level of the surrounding country. They ran from the higher country to points where the rivers were fordable. With some notable exceptions, they were not durable roads, but tracks from the high ground, where the Britons largely resided, to the shipping ports. So persisting and unyielding is popular usage, and so little thought has there ever been of changing the course of a public thoroughfare, that we may well imagine these ancient hollow-ways and ridgeways, from Cornwall to Northumberland, to survive, if not even in some lines of Roman road, at any rate in many a sunken lane or moorland track, in many a field path or right-of-way.

These sunken roads are well illustrated by the remains of a trackway leading through Hazelwood, in the Parish of Avening, still known by the name of the " Old Bristol Road."

[1] The Story of the King's Highway p. 3.

It is, as described above, very irregular and deeply hollowed out by the traffic, in some places being as much as twelve to fifteen feet below the level of the wood through which it passes, and only just wide enough to allow the passage of a loaded animal. Crossing the ancient road over the hills leading from Nailsworth to Avening, it passes through the British Camp, or village, at Ruggers Green, mentioned in Chapter I, and is seen again in the field road to Beverston. Continuing on the high ground, it dipped into the valley, probably at Dodington, as the present main road does, and so on to the port of Bristol. I have been told by those who were living before the making of the Turnpike road from Nailsworth Bridge to Avening Cross in 1823 that strings of horses and donkeys might frequently be seen winding through Hazelwood, over the " Longfords," and, unless that was their destination, on up the old lane, of which traces are still to be seen, to Minchinhampton. Another well-marked hollow-way rises from the Nailsworth valley, and, crossing what is now called the " W Hill," from its zigzag course, leads to Minchinhampton and the Box.

The principal Roman road in the neighbourhood was that leading from Corinium (Cirencester) to the Severn valley, passing over Minchinhampton Common, where traces of it are still to be seen. There is also a lane which crossed the brook near Little Britain farm and passed through the Roman pottery works, for the use of the great villa of Woodchester, and ultimately led to Hampton Common. The trackways mentioned above were also, no doubt, used by the Romans, and it was on altering the course of the old Bristol road that the votive altar mentioned in Chapter III was found.

The earlier history of the Roads under the Tudors and Stuarts is too large a subject to enter on, but it is a most interesting study and I cannot do better than refer those who are desirous of further information to " The Story of the King's Highway," quoted above, which is most interesting and entertaining reading.

The English roads were in an almost incredibly bad state during the 17th and up to the beginning of the 19th century, and this is not to be wondered at considering the manner in which they were repaired. Instead of the modern steam

roller, a "road plough" was frequently employed. Albert
Pell, writing in 1887, says :—

> "People now living may have seen, decaying under
> the walls of the Parish Church, the enormous plough,
> girt and stayed with iron, which, as Spring approached,
> was annually furbished up and brought into the village
> street. For this the owners, or their tenants, acting in
> concert, made up joint teams of six or eight powerful
> horses, and proceeded to the restoration of their high-
> ways by ploughing them up, casting the furrow towards
> the centre, and then harrowing them down to a fairly
> level surface for the summer traffic. Right down to the
> opening of the nineteenth century England had practically
> nothing but soft dirt roads, mended with weak, rotten
> sand and gravel, or with flint or rolling pebbles, con-
> tributed by the farmers, and picked off the arable fields
> by the frozen fingers of rural infants. For all this miserable
> outfit statutable books had to be kept, made up, and
> verified ; a separate rate got out, solemnly allowed by
> Justices of the Peace, and then collected. The whole
> business ended with a wrangle at the Vestry, for which
> the Surveyor fortified himself with a brimming jorum
> of brandy and water." [1]

Turnpike Trusts came into existence about the year 1706,
and during the whole of the 18th century, and in the early
part of the 19th, they were established by thousands, separate
Acts of Parliament being required for each Trust. In these
Acts a certain number of persons of local position and influence
were mentioned by name as the first Trustees, and some also
were ex-officio members. The trustees were empowered to
construct and maintain certain specified lengths of road, and
to levy tolls thereon for a limited term of years, which were
usually extended by a new Act.

The first Turnpike Road Act in this neighbourhood received the Royal assent on March 21st, 1780, and a Meeting
of Trustees was held on March 30th to make arrangements for
carrying it into effect. These Meetings were for many years
held at the Old Lodge on Hampton Common, which was
designated as the first place of meeting in the Act of Parliament. The Chairman at the first, and many subsequent

[1] The Story of the King's Highway, pp. 32-33.

meetings, was Sir Geo. Onesiphorus Paul, mentioned in Chapter VIII., and there are also signatures of others well-known in the neighbourhood at the time. At the first meeting it was decided that the roads sanctioned in the Act should be made in the following order :—

1stly. The road from Tiltups Barn through St. Chloe's grounds to Dudbridge.

2ndly. The road from the bridge at Nailsworth to, or near the Fives Court[1] on Minchinhampton Common.

3rdly. The road from Nurligate on Selsley (Hill) by the Spout to near the Bear Inn in the Parish of Rodborough and from the park stile at Woodchester to join the new road to Frogmarsh.

4thly. The road from Dudbridge through the Buckholt Wood to near the top of Frocester Hill.

5thly. The road from the bridge at Nailsworth by Howcomb and the Wellhill to Minchinhampton Town."

At the next meeting it was agreed to direct Mr Weston to stake out the tracks of the different roads and to plan them for a fee of £32.

On the 19th of April it was ordered that advertisements be inserted in the Gloucester and Birmingham newspapers inviting tenders for making the line of road from Tiltups Inn to Dudbridge, and on the 13th of June the tender of Dennis Edison, of Chester, amounting to £1,400, for making the first line of road, was accepted and ordered to be embodied in a formal agreement. At the same time a Committee was appointed to value the land required for the road, and on the 26th of June they made their report. The valuations range from 20s to 60s per acre per annum, 35s being about the average and the fee simple of the land was computed at 26 years' purchase on the rental. It will readily be imagined that very few were satisfied with the value placed on their land, and eventually Counsel's opinion had to be taken before the matter was finally settled. To provide funds for the expenses of obtaining the Act of Parliament, and for payments on account to the Contractor and for many other expenses, money was advanced by members of the Committee in return

---

[1] The Fives Court was at the Half-Way House Inn and the wall against which the game was played is still to be seen.

for Bonds bearing interest at 5%. During the existence of
the turnpike system, these Bonds were a favourite form of
investment, and very large amounts were raised by these
means all over the country, as, on the security of the revenue
from the turnpikes, they were considered perfectly safe.
Bonds were periodically paid off, but there were still some
remaining when the abolition of the turnpikes extinguished
the security.

Finally, towards the end of the year 1781, the road was
finished and open for traffic, and on the 19th of February,
1782, it was ordered by the Trustees " That an Advertisement
be without delay sent to the Dublin paper, ' St. James's
Chronicle,' ' London Evening Post,' a Bristol, Bath, and
Gloucester newspaper, making public our new road."

The Tolls were fixed as under :—

For every Horse, Mare, Gelding, Mule or other Beast or Cattle drawing any carriage	4d
For every Horse, Mare, etc., not drawing	1d
For every drove of Oxen or other neat Cattle .. .. per score	10d
For Calves, Sheep, or Swine per score	5d
For broad wheeled Waggons or Carts per horse	3d
For narrow wheeled carriages per horse	3½d
For narrow wheeled waggons with four horses, from Nov. 1st to April 30th	2s
For the remainder of the year ..	1s 6d

The tolls were at first let to contractors by public auction
to the highest bidder, but this system gave rise to a considerable amount of fraud, as the bidders made a ring amongst
themselves to keep the prices down. So unsatisfactory was
the bidding sometimes that the Trustees took the collection
of tolls into their own hands, and the gate-keepers were sworn
to give an honest account of all tolls taken. This system did
not work at all satisfactorily, and there were perpetual quarrels
between the Surveyor and the Turnpike Keepers, with the

result that the Trustees had to revert to letting the Tolls by auction.

The Turnpikes did not become established without considerable opposition, and there are in these Minutes accounts of prosecution for damaging the gates and assaulting the keepers. This, however, was nothing to what occurred, principally in South Wales, during the " Rebecca " riots in 1842-43. Armed gangs of men, sometimes disguised as women, assembled at night, destroyed the gates, and pulled down the pike houses, allowing the unfortunate tolltaker only time enough to move his goods into an adjoining field. Carmarthenshire alone had eighty gates destroyed, and in the counties of Pembroke and Cardigan not a gate was left standing. These gangs went by the name of " Rebecca and her children," in allusion to the verse in Genesis (xxiv., 60), in which Rebecca is promised that she shall possess the " Gate " of her enemies. [1]

During the latter part of the 18th century, and the first half of the 19th, the roads and trusts multiplied exceedingly, so much so that the old Borough of Stroud alone had no less than 13 different Trusts, each levying its own tolls, and it was quite possible in a short journey to be compelled to pay at three, or even four, gates. Attempts were made to amalgamate some of the Trusts, where they were most redundant, but little good was done, owing chiefly to the difficulty of adjusting the finances of the different roads, some being much more in debt than others.

The old Turnpike roads were very different to the main roads of the present day, and in an oolite district especially, where only soft stone was available, the surface must have been truly deplorable. The macadam system no doubt effected considerable improvement, but still the unsuitability of the local stone remained, and it was not until the establishment of the railways, that it was possible to procure more suitable stone. Owing to the poverty of the Trusts and the great difficulty of haulage, only a limited quantity of the harder stone could be used on the roads, especially in districts far away from a railway. Many of us can remember, before the coming of the steam roller and the general adoption of suitable material, how heart-breaking it was to drive over a stretch of

[1] For a description of the " Rebecca " Riots see The Story of the King's Highway, pp. 217-220.

road newly metalled, bruising the feet of the horses, and ruining the wheels of the carriages, and how in a wet season the surface of the road was a sea of deep sticky mud ; the present generation is truly fortunate in having the beautiful roads of the present day provided for their use.

The last road made in this district was entirely in the Parish of Avening, and the Act authorising it received the Royal assent May 24th, 1822. It is described in the Act as "A new piece of road to lead from, or from near, the bridge at *Nailsworth*, by or near a place called *Longfords* to a place called *The Cross*, in the Parish of Avening, all in the county of *Gloucester*." This road cut off the old Pack Horse Track through Hazelwood, already mentioned, a new road being made to take its place starting from the Iron Mills.

The abolition of Turnpike Trusts began in 1865, was accelerated by the Act of 1870, and completed about the year 1890. Thousands of miles of " disturnpiked " roads were thus thrown on the rates, causing great resentment, which was to a certain extent mitigated in 1876 by a "Grant in Aid." In 1888 the County Councils were established, and an additional grant was given with the obligation of maintaining the main roads.

By the same local government act the maintenance of the Highways, or secondary roads, was thrown on the District Council. These Highways had frequently been maintained by the Parish, combined with a system of poor relief. Thus a Minchinhampton Vestry Minute in 1826 says :—" Many of the Highways in this Parish requiring great improvement, it is unanimously resolved that the best means of providing for the able poor will be to consolidate the highway rates of this parish, and employ such poor in repairing such highways, and in sloping the Quarries of the Common so as to render them less dangerous ; that the price to be paid by the Parish for labour shall be three-fifths of such sum as shall be named by Mr Smart as a fair compensation, he so calculating as to allow an able labourer, accustomed to such work, to earn ten shillings per week ; that Mr Smart be appointed superintendent and that he bring in his charge for such superintendence at every monthly meeting."

There is but little more to be said as to the roads in our two Parishes. Considering the hilly country in which they are situated, and some other disadvantages, both main roads and Rural Council secondary roads are good andwell maintained.

———————

I here finish the story of the Parishes of Minchinhampton and Avening, and, though I am well aware that there are further details connected with this history which might have been included, yet I hope that this sketch will be of interest to those of my readers who live within the boundaries of the two Parishes or in their neighbourhood.

INDEX